NATIONAL
MINORITY

Alan M. Kent

NATIONAL MINORITY

Francis
Boutle
Publishers

First published by Francis Boutle Publishers
272 Alexandra Park Road
London N22 7BG
Tel/Fax: +44 (0)20 8889 7744
Email: info@francisboutle.co.uk
www.francisboutle.co.uk

ISBN 978 1 903427 90 3

Acknowledgements

The author would like to thank Neil Kennedy and Matthew Spriggs for their insight into the background of this play. I am grateful to Nicholas Williams for providing the imagined sermons. My thanks also to Trevor Cuthbertson and Andy Blake for their input into the development of the text of this play. I am also grateful for the input of Clive Baker, Anna Finch, Sue Ellery (for permitting the use of the music of Brenda Wootton), Hedluv and Passman, Phil Innes, Jonnie Bennett, Elisa Harris and Miracle Theatre.

Biographies

Wesley Griffith – *Edward Cardew, Jake Rowe*
Wesley was brought up in St Ives in Cornwall and studied acting at the Guildford School of Acting. Along with stage performances and a few pieces of film he also records plays and comedy shorts. He is inspired by the work of playwright Harold Pinter whilst his favourite role to date has been Frank Gibbons in a not very well known Noel Coward play – *This Happy Breed*, in which the character ages twenty years over the course of the action. His role in *National Minority* poses an exciting new challenge for him.

Rebecca Hulbert – *Mrs Angela Couch, Alison Heard, Christabelle Trevanion*
Rebecca was born and brought up in Cornwall. She trained at the Royal Welsh College of Music and Drama in acting and has worked in theatre, film, television and radio. She has worked with a variety of theatre companies in Britain as well as Teatro Modus Vivendi in Italy, touring the play *Bloody Poetry* by Howard Brenton. In Cornwall she worked with Miracle Theatre and Cube Theatre. She recently toured with Cube in *After the Accident*, a play that explored the issues around restorative justice, and won the Amnesty International 'Protect the Human' play-writing competition in 2008. She is also a music worker for the charity WILD Young Parents Project.

Daniel Richards – *Stage Manager*

Daniel helped found Falmouth-based theatre company Near-ta Theatre at the age of 16 and went on to work on the majority of their shows. He was part of Miracle Theatre for a year and a half and worked on several productions, including *Cat's Cradle* and *Tartuffe*. He is now co-artistic director of 'Owdyado Theatre, co-writing, producing and performing in *About a Bench*, *Wrongdoing and Wake Up Calls at the Stop-Off Motel* and *Above Bored*. He has worked with Trifle Gathering Productions and Trebiggan Productions and with various Falmouth University film projects, including Dog Bite Film Crew and Cornwall College, as well as with various film makers.

Benjamin Symes – *Piers Trevanion, Trudge*

Benjamin is an actor, director and producer. He has a degree in English Literature and qualifications in Education, Creative Writing and Psychotherapy. He has worked as a carer, clown, teacher and venue manager. He has no formal training in theatre but has acted and directed since he was young, first in the West Kent Youth Theatre. He co-founded Cube Essential Theatre in 2007. Since then he has been its artistic director. Cube has toured extensively and is now resident company at Hall For Cornwall. The company is currently working on a one-man play about fatherhood and an version of *The Crucible* for the Minack. Benjamin has also worked as an actor for Pie-in-Ear, Cscape dance, Miracle Theatre, Bish Bash Bosh, Trifle Gathering and appeared in several episodes of *Doc Martin* (ITV). He performed in Alan M. Kent's *A Mere Interlude*. He has directed over 40 student/community shows and *Carmen* for Duchy Opera and *A Midsummer Night's Dream* for Platform (Hall for Cornwall).

Jason Squibb – *Director*

Jason is a producer, director and actor. He is Artistic Director of Collective Arts Ltd, specialising in large scale productions, such as the Falmouth Charter celebrations and a play about Admiral Nelson for the SeaBritain Festival. Jason has worked on a number of adaptations from the Cornish medieval dramatic tradition. He directed the *Life of St Meriasek* and Alan M. Kent's *Bewnans Peran*. Since 2007 he has also performed with Miracle Theatre and was cast as Rev. Rupert Longfellow in Miracle's first feature film *Tin*, and has gone on to play many vicars, including the Rev. Clarence Odgers in the BBC's *Poldark*. He has also performed with Trebiggan Productions. His TV and film roles include work on *Doc Martin* (Buffalo Pictures), *Skynt – the musical*, *The Car* (BBC), *The Bill* (Thames) and *Steps* (HTV/Westernlights). Jason has also worked as a motion capture actor with the Moving Picture Company.

Alan M. Kent – *Playwright*

Alan M. Kent was a born in St Austell. He studied at the Universities of Cardiff and Exeter gaining a Doctorate in Cornish and Anglo-Cornish literature. He is a lecturer in Literature with the Open University and Visiting Lecturer in Celtic Studies at the University of Coruña, Galicia, As well as being a dramatist, he is also an acclaimed novelist and poet. His plays include translations of the Cornish Mystery Play Cycle known as *Ordinalia*, *Nativitas Christi*, *Oogly es Sin*, *The Tin Violin*, *Surfing Tommies*, *A Mere Interlude*, *The Beast of Bodmin Moor* and *Bewmans Peran*. Recent academic works have included *The Theatre of Cornwall: Space, Place, Performance*, *Towards a Cornish Philosophy* and an edition of the *Theatre Works of Charles Causley*. His most recent volume of poetry is *Interim Nation*, and he is editor of *Wave Hub: New Poetry from Cornwall*. He is the Series Editor of Francis Boutle Publisher's collection of anthologies of Lesser Used Languages and co-editor of *New Perspectives in Cornish and Celtic Studies*.

The first production of *National Minority* was staged by Gwary Teg
Theatre and performed in Cornwall in October 2015.

Actor 1 – Male

PIERS TREVANION – 35 years old: tweed suit, tie and loafers.

TRUDGE – 25 years old: unshaven, low-slung trousers, hoodie and gold
chains

Actor 2 – Female

MRS ANGELA COUCH – 40 years old: black dress, white apron, bonnet and
black shoes.

ALISON HEARD – 27 years old: wears clothes that make her look older
than she is, pearls, flat shoes and hair in a French plait.

CHRISTABELLE TREVANION – 32 years old: white dress, ribbon in her hair,
stockings and stylish shoes.

Actor 3 – Male

EDWARD CARDEW – 30 years old: bearded, suited and a red waistcoat.

JAKE ROWE – 25 years old: dark-haired, bearded, jeans, a white top and a
black scarf.

A note on the next

The play is intended to be a three-hander where the doubling and tripling aids the audience's understanding. It can however, also be played by more than three actors. Costume changes should always be made in front of the audience. Imagined initial sections of *The Sherwood Sermons* should be recorded and played during the transitions between scenes. The Cornish-language version merges into the English translation.

Only Hope was left within her unbreakable house,
she remained under the lip of the jar, and did not
fly away. Before [she could], Pandora replaced the
lid of the jar. This was the will of aegis-bearing
Zeus the Cloudgatherer.

From Hesiod's *Works and Days*, c.700 BCE

'Why should Cornishmen learn Cornish? There is no money in it, it
serves no practical purpose, and the literature is scanty and of no great
originality or value. The question is a fair one, the answer is simple.
Because they are Cornishmen.'

From Henry Jenner, *Handbook of the Cornish Language*, London: David
   Nutt, 1904.

NATIONAL
MINORITY

Prologue

The first thing we hear is Actor 1 saying the following lines as the character of Trudge. *These are thoughtful and laconic.*

Trudge When you're a kid, they tell you to grow up, get a job, get married, get a house, have kids and that's it. (*Beat*). But the truth is that the world is so much stranger than that. It's so much darker, so much more mad and crazy... and so much better.

Act One

Scene One

The library at Rosenannon – a large country house in mid-Cornwall – in February 1901. Oak-panelling would surround the room, but this is not shown. Instead, upstage centre are a pair of curtained French windows. Upstage right is a tapestry showing the dominating arms of the Trevanion family: sable, a yellow cross in the first quarter: a Cornish chough, argent beaked and legged gules; in the second quarter: a text "T in the third and fourth quarters: a crescent all of the third. Next to it is a sturdy grandfather clock.

Upstage left, a representative tall bookshelf, containing dusty, brown, leather-covered books and folios of various sizes. On stage left is a fireplace, with two fire dogs and a black companion set. Next to the companion set, a basket of logs. The fire is lit. Stage right is a framed wooden door leading to the imagined entrance hall of the house. By the door is a coat-stand.

Downstage centre is a long, polished table, with three, straight-backed matching chairs behind it. On the table, an oil-lamp, a model of a lugger fishing boat, a wooden reading rest, some deeds and rolled-up maps, haphazard piles of books (some bookmarked; some left face down and open) and a stationery set. Above the table is a glass chandelier. On the floor is a large, brightly-decorated Axminster rug. The room has a faded elegance.

Noise of people arriving is heard in the hallway. The housekeeper MRS ANGELA COUCH *enters the door, and shivers slightly. Her hand finds an imagined switch on the wall and she turns it on. Lights come up on the stage. She looks across to the fire, turns back out and addresses someone in the hall.*

ANGELA My gar... Brrrr... Weather idn ut? Never knawed of anything like ut. Now, tis just in 'ere Mr Cardew... Not a room that's used very much these days – but you'll soon see the lie of it.

A low voice is heard from the hallway. It is EDWARD CARDEW.

EDWARD Coming. Just fetching my suit-case inside.

ANGELA You'm a'right my lover, my 'andsome... my bewdie... Come us you on in ere. Got a nice fire goin' fur ee. You'll soon warm up.

EDWARD *appears through the door. He is carrying a suitcase and a briefcase. He pauses, looks around and decides to put down his briefcase on the table. He places the suitcase on the floor beneath it on the Axminster rug.*

EDWARD I say, Mrs... ah...?

ANGELA Mrs Couch...

EDWARD What a splendid room, Mrs Couch! What I'd give for a library like this in my own residence. Mine is not much more than a cupboard.

ANGELA Well, Mr Trevanion d'like me t'keep ut somethun like ut... Come over 'ere – beside the fire... Warm yerself up a bit Mr Carew, eh? Toasty see. I never knawed a February like ut. S'cold like – an rainun' and sleet all the time yew...

EDWARD Please, call me Edward... Let's not stand on ceremony, eh?

ANGELA Edward...? Well, let me take your coat, Mr Card... *(laughs)* Edward.

3

ANGELA *helps* EDWARD *remove his coat, and she hangs it on the coat-stand.* EDWARD *moves towards the fire, his hands feeling for its warmth.*

EDWARD Lovely...

ANGELA Proper job, idn ut? That'll warm ee up a bit, my lover.

EDWARD Thank you. It's most welcome. Much as I like travel by train, the stations of God's Wonderful Railway are always cold and draughty. St Austell's no different to Paddington in that way.

ANGELA Tell me, how was your trip down then?

EDWARD One word for it – long. I forget just how far away Cornwall is sometimes...

ANGELA Well, we'm brave an' distant from Lunnon, true enough. Now where es ut you'd'work again? Mr Trevanion he did tell me...

EDWARD The British Museum.

ANGELA Aaawww. Now that do sound posh. Brit-ish Mu-se-um. 'Andsome that be, I spect.

EDWARD It's nothing remarkable really. Just a lot of pen-pushing clods cataloguing everything the British empire's stolen from everywhere else.

ANGELA Now I'm sure tis more than that my lover, my 'andsome...

EDWARD A little more Mrs Couch – but not much... The English started with places like Cornwall, Wales and Ireland – and then moved on to Egypt, Iraq and Mesopotamia. Nothing's sacred once the imperial boot has landed. Anything from the past is up for grabs for speculation and interpretation.

A pause.

ANGELA So, what is ut you do up there zactly then?

EDWARD Manuscripts. I am Keeper of the Manuscript collection.

ANGELA Aw, yes. Piers – ah, Mr Trevanion, said that was your purpose in coming here... But now, even though you'm a gentleman an that... I'n trace a bit ov Cornish in you. Now am I right m'andsome or am I wrong?

4

EDWARD You have a shrewd ear, Mrs Couch. I was born in St Columb Major...

ANGELA (*delighted*) See, I knawed ov ut. You'n take the man out ov Cornwall, but you cen't take Cornwall out ov the man.

EDWARD Very true.

ANGELA Well, my Uncle Royston just last week comed back from mining over Colorado. Been over there ten years ee ave. You wudn' knaw he'd gone. Still speaks un broad. Ee d'say since I been workin' ere at Rosenannon that I'm proper cut up now, but I soon put ee right.

EDWARD Plenty of mines've gone scat in Cornwall now but Fowey Consuls still seem to be doin' well for the Trevanions. From what I hear, at least...

ANGELA I got to thank my lucky stars tis that way really. I mean things ent good elsewhere are um? I'd'hear ov ut – people with no money down west beggin' in the streets an' eatun ov limpets off the beach... Eatun' ov limpets coz they got nothun more... Well tidn' never right is ut Mr Cardew? Tidn' never right in this day an age. (*conspiratorially*). A lot ov folk round here d'knock the Trevanions (*she points to the coat of arms*) but they've always invested well. Years in tin, copper and exports yew – but lately in clay – an' doin' very well from ut, so they d'say. (*Beat*) Now hear ov me chitterin on like there idn' naw tomorra. You dun't want t'be hearin' of Mr Trevanion's housekeeper like that do ee now? You want t'be gettin' on with what you'm here fur.

EDWARD Well, yes, but I do like to hear your take on things Mrs Couch...

ANGELA Ange. Call me Ange. Edward...

EDWARD Ange... Now will Piers be back later so I can perhaps make a start?

ANGELA Aw es. Not long t'all. In the meantime, I'll take your case up to your room shall I? Tis nice. Western facing. Lovely sunset. You'n look right out over the bay. I'll pop a warming pan in the sheets fur ee too. Keep the chill out ov a winter night.

ANGELA *picks up* EDWARD's *suitcase.*

ANGELA You be a'right here?

EDWARD Of course. A room full of books. Books are my life... Ange.

5

ANGELA Right you are sir... I'll leave ee to ut.

ANGELA leaves and takes out the suitcase with her. EDWARD smiles to himself. He is left to his own devices in the library. He goes over to the bookshelf and scans a few of the titles. He picks out one book, looks at the cover and flicks through it. He nods at what he is reading, then puts the title back carefully. He peers up and around to show some of the size of the library. He goes over to the French windows and pulls back a section of curtain to look outside. As he does this, the grandfather clock strikes five o'clock. The striking of the clock makes him jump, and he compares the time on the clock with his own wrist-watch. His eye catches the model lugger on the table and he goes over to it and picks it up. He holds it up to the light, admiring its lines and shape, feeling the wood.

From the hallway a door slams, and voices are heard. The voices are of ANGELA, and PIERS TREVANION.

ANGELA Evening, sir. Everything fine down Consuls?

PIERS Surprisingly so – considering... Mrs Couch, be a dear and fetch me a brandy, will you?

ANGELA Mr Cardew's arrived... He's in the library. I've made his room ready.

PIERS Cardew? Of course. I had it in my diary he'd be coming today... What with the works and everything I'd completely forgotten. Better bring a bottle in.

ANGELA And Mrs Trevanion? Down from Bath tonight do ee think?

PIERS One hopes so.

Expecting the entry of either of them into the library, EDWARD puts down the model and sits at one of the chairs. He starts to unpack his briefcase, and places these items on the table. The items include a note-book, a larger hardback book (Bibliotheca Cornubiensis) and a magnifying glass. EDWARD peers into the glass which increases the size of his left eye. At this moment, PIERS bursts into the room, opening wide the door.

PIERS Mr Carew. Piers Trevanion. A pleasure to meet you. Welcome to Rosenannon.

PIERS makes his way over to EDWARD and vigorously shakes his hand. EDWARD stands to greet him.

6

EDWARD Very pleased to meet you. Thank you for hosting me.

PIERS Mrs Couch been looking after you, I trust?

EDWARD Very well indeed. That fire's warmed me up nicely.

PIERS Well, something else should warm you up in a moment. I've asked Mrs Couch to fetch some brandy in. You do partake I trust? Not one of these teetotal Methodees…

EDWARD (*nervously*) Of course. A drop will go down rather well.

PIERS Now let's see now. When did you first write to me about this matter?

EDWARD Before Christmas I think.

PIERS I'm damned sorry it's taken this long to get you down here old boy.

EDWARD Well, I'm thankful for you replying to my initial letter. Some people don't, you know.

PIERS Your name is held in much esteem, though I must admit I'm not really a literary man. You can probably tell from all the dust in here. Mrs Couch gets angry with me but I instruct her not to bother. We normally show guests into the drawing room and not in here.

EDWARD It's quite a collection. I had a quick look.

PIERS Do you think so? Books, I'm afraid, are lost on me. I'm more the sporting type. Always have been. My father though, liked to spend time in here. He was bookish… Maybe he would have known…

At this moment, ANGELA *comes in with a tray, holding a decanter of brandy and two glasses.*

PIERS Ah. Splendid.

ANGELA Shall I pour, sir?

PIERS Please do. Don't be sparing. Mr Cardew and I have much to discuss.

ANGELA *pours a sizeable quantity into each glass but then catches* PIERS' *eye which encourages her to top them up further.* PIERS *picks up the two glasses and hands one to* EDWARD.

ANGELA *gives a small curtsey.*

7

ANGELA I'll leave the decanter.

PIERS *nods.* ANGELA *exits.*

PIERS *holds his glass in the air, ready for a toast.*

PIERS Well, I suppose this ought to be to 'the undiscovered country'…

EDWARD The undiscovered country? Cornwall?

PIERS From *Hamlet* I believe. Something lodged itself in there (*pointing at his head*) from my school days…

PIERS *and* EDWARD *toast and drink.*

PIERS The undiscovered country.

EDWARD The undiscovered country.

PIERS Damned good, that stuff. My father had a keg or two brought back from Roscoff. It's lasted years.

EDWARD A fine blend. And to pick up your point, I suppose, yes, I am after the undiscovered country. Or rather the undiscovered manuscript…

PIERS (*laughs*) Well, I have to say I was intrigued by your letter. To think that we have something of antiquarian interest here at Rosenannon.

EDWARD We shall see. I am looking everywhere, Piers. Manuscripts turn up in the oddest places you know. Jumble sales, garden sheds… There was one I found in a flea market in Truro.

PIERS And is it only manuscripts you seek?

EDWARD No. Not at all. With Cornish, I have been collecting all over the place. Last summer, I spent time in Penwith recording old people. I was listening to the way certain words were pronounced.

PIERS And did any of them have the old tongue about them? I thought it had died out a century or more ago. Dolly Pentreath and all that…

EDWARD *takes another sip of brandy.*

EDWARD You'd be surprised. You really would. The language is like a sub-soil. English is laid down over the top but scratch the surface a bit – and it's there… rather like your china clay on the top of Hensbarrow.

PIERS I see. Now, do you think anyone will want to revive this Cornish language? I must say, I was thinking today what a damn foolhardy endeavour that might be.

EDWARD There are some already. We have grammars, lexicons, dictionaries. The dialect of English in Cornwall is also a huge resource.

PIERS Well I never. Hobby types are they? More time on their hands than they know what to do with, eh?

EDWARD (*guardedly*) I find they seek themselves – to come to know their past a little better.

PIERS You know such people?

EDWARD I must confess... I probably *am* one of them. I have been encouraged to write a *Handbook* – and if I find what I am looking for here – well, it may help things along...

PIERS Quite. I didn't mean to...

EDWARD (*laughs*) ...to say it's a waste of time?

PIERS No. More about why we might need the language again?

EDWARD I see.

PIERS I mean – do you imagine a future where we might be – ha – bi-lingual?

EDWARD I don't necessarily think it will happen – but it might be good to think it might happen. We are, after all, one of the minority groups of this land...

PIERS Intriguing. Most intriguing. You've certainly got me thinking Mr Cardew.

PIERS *finishes his brandy.*

PIERS Did you want to start looking tonight?

EDWARD Oh no. I think it's probably too late now...

PIERS Maybe... and Mrs Couch will be preparing supper.

EDWARD (*with great enthusiasm*). But do let me show you this. It's what I was referring to in my letter. Here, see...

EDWARD *beckons over* PIERS *to the table and opens the larger hardback book* (Bibliotheca Cornubiensis). *With his finger he then points to a reference.*

PIERS What's this?

EDWARD Volume 2 of Bibliotheca Cornubiensis by G.C. Boase and W.P. Courtney ...1882...

PIERS The title?

EDWARD (*speedily*) It's a listing. Shows every manuscript and book written about Cornwall – written or published up until 1882. George Clement Boase. Born in Penzance in 1827. Died 1897 in Lewisham. A successful banker for much of his life. A trip to Australia, and then back to edit this... Three volumes, you know. Courtney – that's William Prideaux... said that section had been collated by Boase – and that he had no notion of it.

PIERS Which section?

EDWARD *points to a specific part of the book.*

EDWARD Here... where I'm pointing... Read across.

PIERS (*aloud, but tentative*) Sermons in Cornish... and English. Preached by Reverend Joseph Sherwood... at St Ives, Marazion and Penzance 1680. MSS. penes Charles Trevanion, esq. Rosenannon.

EDWARD You see. Boase says it's here.

PIERS Charles was my grandfather. (*Beat*). How did they end up here? I mean they were preached down west – not here...

EDWARD In two hundred years a manuscript may travel many miles.

PIERS And 1680 – the date?

EDWARD Yes... The date of the manuscript, at least – according to Boase. They might, of course, be earlier...

PIERS Not long after the Civil War...

EDWARD Indeed. Somewhere near the end of the reign of Charles II.

PIERS And in Cornish *and* in English?

EDWARD *nods.*

EDWARD Written at a time of language shift no doubt... St Ives, Marazion, Penzance – they'd still have some Cornish speakers left. Some of the congregation might hear them in Cornish. Others might prefer the English...

PIERS In the same sermon?

EDWARD Who knows? Maybe one after the other. Maybe separate sermons for each group of speakers. We simply don't know.

EDWARD *downs the last of his brandy and places the glass onto the table.* PIERS *is still engrossed in the book.* EDWARD *walks around the library.*

EDWARD You don't recall seeing them anywhere then? Even as a child?

PIERS As I said, I barely come in here. When I was a child, the library was for grandfather alone really. It was his domain. The only thing I knew – in a literary sense – was *Hamlet*.

EDWARD I must work systematically through the room. Is there an order? A catalogue perhaps?

PIERS Nothing as far as I know. (*Beat*). And if you find it?

EDWARD We will know more. I mean it may not change much – most of our knowledge of the language is drawn from the great dramas – *Ordinalia, Bewnans Meriasek, The Creation of the World...*

PIERS Plays, you say?

EDWARD Cornwall's principal literary mode. Every parish had a play celebrating its saint and his or her achievements. If not, then they'd dramatise the Bible – from the Creation to the Resurrection. Rosenannon – the estate here – probably had a playing place – the arena in which they were performed.

PIERS I never knew.

EDWARD Most people don't. Instead they concrete over their history as if it were nothing of consequence. Or else encourage day-trippers.

PIERS But these sermons? Why them? Short, aren't they? Correct me if I'm wrong but surely you should be looking to find more of the plays?

EDWARD Undoubtedly there are more of the plays out there. Perhaps we should be looking elsewhere – Wales, Brittany, the Vatican even... But sometimes, it is the smaller text that holds the greatest reward.

Boase doesn't describe them. He just notes their existence. They may be long. They may be short. No-one knows.

PIERS Did he come here? This chap Boase?

EDWARD Must've I suppose. Must've known. I mean he's right about just about everything in there.

EDWARD points at the copy of Bibliotheca Cornubiensis.

PIERS *(perceptively)* We are walking amongst ghosts.

EDWARD Sometimes, that is all there is. Literary history is littered with supposed texts, things that have succumbed to mildew or damp, and so have been lost. My days – Mr Trevanion – are spent following such dead ends. They give me life.

PIERS All the more reason for you to be successful here then. Please – I want you to know – take as much time as you need… Open every volume if it helps. Scrutinize everything. There are no skeletons in the closet here.

EDWARD Thank you. I much appreciate that.

There is a knock at the door. ANGELA *enters.*

ANGELA Sir, supper's ready.

PIERS Wonderful.

ANGELA I thought in the banquet room tonight sir…

PIERS Of course. If we can't entertain a guest such as Mr Cardew in there, then who can we entertain?

ANGELA All ready for the first course. Chicken Soup.

ANGELA *leaves through the door.* PIERS *extends his hand showing the way.*

PIERS Please… after you…

EDWARD *nods and heads to the door.*

PIERS The Sherwood Sermons then… Nice ring to it.

EDWARD Even better if I can locate them.

PIERS I'm sure you will sir. I am sure you will. Shall we?

EDWARD *and* PIERS *exit the library. As the transition occurs we hear the*
following sermon in Cornish, voiced by EDWARD:

EDWARD Ima Tomas Aquyn, henwys doctor angelicus gans an egglos a
Rome, ow teclaria fatell yw res porres the pup creatur human rag y
salvacion bos obedyent then pabe a Rome. An pab brassa bythquath a
veu byttegyns, Gregory Mer, ny rug eff kemeras thotha y honyn power
an par na rag eff a elwys y honyn servus servorum Dei, an servant a
servigy Du. Gregory a vnderstandyas in ta an lavar na a Grist y honyn
in vgansves chapter a Mathew: Non ita erit inter vos: sed quicumque
voluerit inter vos major fieri, sit vester minister: et qui voluerit inter
vos primus esse, erit vester servus hen ew the styrria, 'Ny vith indella
genowgh why, saw pynagul a garsa bos an brassa in agys mysk why,
bethans eff agas servant; ha penagul a vo whensys the vos an kynsa
ahanowgh, re bo eff agys keth.'

[Thomas Aquinas called Doctor Angelicus by the Roman church
declares that obedience to the Pope is utterly necessary for the salva-
tion of every human creature. The greatest of Popes, however,
Gregory the Great did not take unto himself such power, for he called
himself servus servorum Dei, the servant of the servants of God.
Gregory understood the saying of Christ himself in the twentieth
chapter of Matthew: Non ita erit inter vos: sed quicumque voluerit
inter vos major fieri, sit vester minister: et qui voluerit inter vos
primus esse, erit vester servus; that is to say 'It will not be so among
you, but whoever wishes to be the greatest among you, let him be your
servant, and who wishes to be first among you, let him be your slave.']

Scene Two

Lights up on the library at Rosenannon House. It is the same kind of
February day as in Scene one, except that the action now takes place in the
present day. This is evident from the clothes and language of the two
characters who enter the room: JAKE ROWE *and* TRUDGE. *Nothing in the*
room should be altered. EDWARD'*s briefcase and items on the table should*
remain exactly where he placed them.

From hereon, it does not matter that properties from one period remain on
stage as the drama flicks between two different times. Thus there are no
anachronisms as the play progresses. Properties will simply assemble on the
table.

The door opens and TRUDGE *enters.*

TRUDGE Christ on a bike! What a fuggin' hovel... It looks like Bilbo Baggins just packed for Mordor last week. We should have a decorating party. You know – few spliffs, that cheap kick-arse Czechoslovakian lager from Aldi, some decent tunes, few bottles of paint stripper from B&Q and Bob's yer uncle. Full-on make-over. DIY SOS. Right on, yew.

JAKE *follows him in carrying a black satchel, inside of which is laptop.*

JAKE It's Frodo, Trudge, y'tool.

TRUDGE Wha'? Put it on YouTube. Two hobbits enter an old country house. What happened next will stun you.

JAKE Frodo. Not Bilbo y'idiot. Bilbo goes to Erebor. Frodo's the one who goes to Mordor. Gollum. Ring. Lava. Remember?

TRUDGE Matter do ut? Whatever the fug you say... *(sarcastic)* Dr Jake Rowe. Professor of Hobbiton Studies at the University of Rivendell...

JAKE And I'm not a doctor yet. I've more of this research to do before I get there.

TRUDGE They'm still midget cunts who have hairy feet an' live in places like this.

A pause. Both of the young men tentatively explore the room, looking at the objects within it. JAKE *picks up the boat and admires it in the same way that* EDWARD *did.*

TRUDGE Whas' tha?

JAKE A lugger. My uncle runned one out ov Meva. Bewdies they were. Traditional. Built by hand.

JAKE *takes off his satchel and unpacks his laptop. He places it on the desk and presses the power button on.* TRUDGE *goes over to the French windows and pulls back the curtain a little so he can look out.*

JAKE Knawin you, you'd probably finish the lager soon as and then neck the paint stripper.

TRUDGE It's like that all the time up St Dennis. Boys up there cen't tell the difference. Anti-depressants. Ritolin. Sambuca. Paint stripper. Naw difference t'all. Then, what the fuck do ee do when you'm facing

14

a waste-to-power cancer-causin' incinerator every day ov yer miserable life. May as well make the moast of ut.

JAKE Don't you realise how lucky we are to get in here? This was the old Trevanion seat.

TRUDGE (*Beat*) Lucky to get *out* more like.

JAKE I had to get a letter of introduction from my tutor. For them to even let us in like. Be careful. Don't break anything.

TRUDGE *ignores what* JAKE *is saying and instead, goes over to the coat of arms and admires it. Quick as, he pulls a mobile phone out of his pocket and takes a picture of himself with the coat of arms in the background.*

TRUDGE Look. What a selfie! Cool... (*He shows the image to* JAKE). See I got the little chough in an' all. I'll whack that on Facebook laters.

JAKE *turns to admire the coat of arms.*

JAKE That's their coat of arms. Probably made centuries ago. The Trevanions were set up when Charles II was back on the throne. They'd supported un see – during the Civil War.

TRUDGE (*sniffs*) Knawed ut. See – more people kiss-arsing royalty. Still, uf ut do get ee somewhere like this, then I s'pause tis worth ut. Eh – where've she gone anyway?

JAKE Who?

TRUDGE That Alison. Her who you wuz talkin' to when I was parking the van.

JAKE She's gone to the site office – it's in a portakabin outside. She said t'go on in. Turn right an into the library. She was right though wudn' she about ut being a time capsule? I mean look at ut all...

TRUDGE *is contemplating something else. He rubs his chin with his right hand.*

TRUDGE I'd do her.

JAKE Eh?

TRUDGE I said I'd do her. She's a bit ov alright ent she? Bit of a PAWG but might ask her out in a minute. She's classy. Might take her out Newquay for a curry or somethun'.

15

JAKE (*laughing to himself*). Classy? What, like you?

TRUDGE Me? Course I'm fuckin classy. Got classy written all over me mate.

JAKE Yes – tattooed on your arse more like.

TRUDGE Look – I'm just saying I like her – thaas' all.

JAKE She's *very* National Trust. Bit Green Wellie. Wax jacket and that.

TRUDGE What? An' I'm not?

JAKE You – Trudge – well, you'm more national distrust ent ee? Face it – you'm a goon from up St Dennis.

TRUDGE Snob.

JAKE Knob.

TRUDGE Git.

JAKE Twat.

TRUDGE You never used t'be like this at school…

JAKE No. Well, things have moved on ent um?

TRUDGE Yeah – now you'm at Uni an' reading for your Ph.D in Twattishness. Is that one of the admission criteria down Tremough is ut? (*moving his arm in the air as he emphasises the following five words*). Must be a complete twat.

JAKE Dun't matter though, do ut Trudge? You'm still me mate.

A pause.

TRUDGE I s'pause so, y'bugger. Anyway, what did ee say to tell she again? What am I?

JAKE Don't you ever listen to a word I say? We discussed this in the van. You'm my "research assistant".

As he says the words "research assistant" JAKE makes the appropriate inverted commas in the air. TRUDGE does the same thing when he speaks.

TRUDGE "Research assistant"? What do I have to do?

JAKE Nothing – yet.

TRUDGE Do I have to "research"?

16

JAKE Sort ov.

TRUDGE With what?

JAKE Nothing. We're just doing a bit of investigating – thaas' all. I needed to see the place where Edward Cardew worked. I want to walk in his footsteps so to speak.

TRUDGE Thaas' who your thesis is on yeah?

JAKE Yeah. The provisional title is 'Reframing Edward Cardew: Cornish Language Pioneer and Nation Builder'. If it weren't fur him we wudn' be no national minority today...

TRUDGE Comed ere did a?

JAKE Yes. In 1901. Bit of a mystery really...

From his usual quasi-rapper / 'cool' stance, TRUDGE *appears to go stiff.*

TRUDGE Hark. Thaas' the front door. She's comin' back.

TRUDGE *moves across the room and sets himself up in a sexy position, leaning against the fire-place.*

JAKE What're you doing?

TRUDGE Watch and learn... watch and learn... The master is at work.

The door opens and ALISON HEARD *walks in. She has the breezy confidence of someone at the top of her game.*

ALISON (*enthusiastic*) You found it okay then?

JAKE Yes – thanks. No probs.

ALISON Well, it's bit dusty I know – but the Trust has big plans for Rosenannon. It's an estate we've had our eye on for some time. Lanhydrock's thinking it could become one of our biggest attractions in Cornwall. Mid-Cornwall. Not far from the Eden Project. Amazing gardens and views of the coast. Beautiful lake. The jewel in the crown, so to speak.

TRUDGE (*under his breath*). Eden Project. What a big bleddy nothun that is...

ALISON *and* JAKE *momentarily stop talking to hear him. When he realises this,* TRUDGE *beams a smile back at them.* ALISON *and* JAKE *turn back from* TRUDGE *to face each other again.*

JAKE So it's official? The National Trust own it now?

ALISON Yes – as of last week. When we e-mailed the ink wasn't quite dry but it's all done and dusted now.

TRUDGE arranges his body into another position. This should echo one of PIERS' stances from Scene One.

JAKE This place. Do you know much about it?

ALISON Well, we're researching now.

At the word 'researching' TRUDGE makes his move.

TRUDGE Let me introduce myself. I am a research assistant. I do research.

ALISON And you are?

JAKE *(slightly panicked)* This is... er... Trudge. He's my assistant. Helps me with my research. Do you remember? I said he'd be coming along with me.

TRUDGE Delighted to meet you ma'am...

ALISON giggles. TRUDGE takes out his mobile and snaps a picture of ALISON and JAKE. He looks at the image and smiles. ALISON and JAKE's conversation halts again. When TRUDGE puts the mobile in his pocket, they carry on again.

ALISON You were saying?

JAKE Um... Yes... So are you in charge here then?

ALISON At the moment... It's an enormous project. We've got grant funding bids in with everyone – Heritage Lottery, Europe, Central Government. Fingers crossed we'll be open in about five years.

JAKE *(surprised)* That's how long the restoration will take?

ALISON Depends. Could be longer. Could be shorter. Depends on what we find. The foundations definitely need work, we know that. Then there's the tower. It's of pock granite so that'll need fixing. Exciting though eh?

TRUDGE Very.

ALISON and JAKE look over at TRUDGE. She is slightly unnerved by him.

18

ALISON (*slightly breathless*) Now, what do you need today? We've got all your introductory notes and background checks. I suppose you want to see this.

Slowly ALISON *moves over to the table and picks up* EDWARD'*s briefcase.*

JAKE (*in awe*) Is that it?

TRUDGE Is that what?

JAKE (*excitedly*) This is Cardew's briefcase. The one he brought here. It's said he used it for absolutely everything. See – it's even got his initials on it – EC... Look...

TRUDGE *examines it and looks distinctly unimpressed.*

ALISON And if I'm right, the objects on the table there – they are all Cardew's as well. See, here's his notebook. That should be of interest to you. And this is his copy of...

JAKE ...the second volume of *Bibliotheca Cornubiensis*, just as you said on the phone.

ALISON Yes – I suppose we ought to have an exhibition. I mean his contribution's quite famous now isn't it?

JAKE Very. He was the founder of so much.

TRUDGE Our modern state even... (*assuming Chinese Communist Party rhetoric*) The Great Leader... The Chosen One.

ALISON Well, you're at liberty to research as you please. I suppose he'd found some books in here somewhere. It is quite a collection. (*She rummages in her jacket*). Ooo – got a text from the restoration architect. Better get back to the office. If you need anything you can find me there. Toilet's in the hall – third door on the right. Tea and coffee in the portakabin too. Can't swear on the state of the milk though... Let me know what you find.

JAKE *is about to speak but is interrupted by* TRUDGE.

TRUDGE Will do. I'll show you all my re-search...

ALISON (*slightly horrified*) I – ah – look forward to it.

ALISON *leaves.*

TRUDGE (*with satisfaction*) See.

JAKE See what?

TRUDGE She likes me.

JAKE How do you know?

TRUDGE Intuition. The way she was looking at me.

JAKE No she wun't. She was probably wondering who the knobber was standing next to the fire like some kind of paedo.

TRUDGE I like the way she speaks. Her language. Where did she go school?

JAKE Truro High School for Girls I think.

TRUDGE I knawed ut. Class written all over her. Better class of maid in Truro. I sees um down Bunters. The rest from Redruth or Newquay – right munters. But Truro maids – class.

JAKE Dream on, if I wuz you.

TRUDGE She'll be putty in my hand by the end of the day. You'll see. (*Beat*). So, that case – is tha' wha' we've comed here for?

JAKE Well, it's one reason I admit. But there's others too. Just to be in this place – where he worked. It's the closest I've got to him.

TRUDGE Stop being s'gay.

JAKE *ignores him and continues.*

JAKE I mean, when you're researching someone's life – you can feel their presence. It's like they're in the here and now. Time-travelling.

TRUDGE Sounds like Dr Who to me. (*Beat*). I mean, why the hell did ee come here anyway? From what you've told me, most of the language stuff was all goin' on in the west.

JAKE That, pard, is what we'm going to find out.

TRUDGE *moves energetically around the room.*

TRUDGE Come on then, professor, tell me a bit more about this Edward Cardew. How the hell did you end up writing about ee anyway?

JAKE Hard to say why anyone ends up writing about anything. I just felt he needed a reassessment – in the light of the new Assembly and everything.

TRUDGE How come?

JAKE Well, all those years ago, he was the one who first proposed Cornwall should go it alone... Home Rule... have its own parliament. He didn't know it as devolution but he'd understand what's happening. Cardew was in there from the start. He did so many things.

TRUDGE *stops to face* JAKE.

TRUDGE Like what?

JAKE *becomes more animated, circling* TRUDGE. *He gestures with his hands*

JAKE For one thing, he wrote the *Handbook of the Cornish Language*.

JAKE *throws* TRUDGE *a copy.* TRUDGE *catches it, reads it disinterestedly.*

JAKE For another, he formed Cowethas Celto-Kernewek. This was the Cornish Celtic Society. And although he was working for much of the time in London – at the British Museum – it was there and in other libraries that he started to search for the Cornish manuscripts. I mean there were people in the past who had a go – Keigwin, Williams, Jago and so on – but Cardew's the man who put it all together. Then there was the Celtic conference in Truro in 1898. He's the one who got Cornwall accepted as a Celtic Nation. Justified it by saying there was enough knowledge of traditional Cornish to make the claim valid. He understood we were a national minority before any other buggers even thought about ut.

TRUDGE Hold it. Hold it. You'm chitterin on like some kind of lawyer. From what you've told me before, I thought he was more ov a translator than a politician.

JAKE He was both. And you're right. He began to translate all the surviving Cornish-language texts. He made an immeasurable contribution.

TRUDGE Alright – but why bother t'ave another geek at un? I mean it's not like you're goin'to find some letter claiming that a liked dressing up in women's underwear. I can see ov un naw – in his suspenders with a copy of a Cornish-English dictionary strapped t'his crotch.

JAKE I know. I know that. It's more to do with the narrative. There's a certain view of him: a bit rosey-tinted I d'reckon. I want to have another look at everything. Find the truth. This summer I'm going through all the correspondence at the British Library.

21

TRUDGE Jesus. You mad bugger. Dun't you ever wish your life was more simple? Be a bit more like me. Come home from work... have a beer, put on FIFA 2014 on the X-box, order a Chinese from Dy-nasty, have a geek at some BBW internet porn, try fur a wank, go pub for a few pints of Doom Bar. twat somebody who's won on the bandit and come ome an' chillax...

JAKE Not really. Besides there's a couple of flaws in your argument. One, you dun't fucking work. Two, last time you twatted somebody on the bandits you wuz given an all year ban up Social Club.

TRUDGE *plays it as a court-room drama, pacing and completing dramatic turns.*

TRUDGE First point of correction sir. The year ban wuz fur swearin in front of minors durin' Feast Week. An' that wus over Indian Queen Club. I got six months for the bandits. The fucker I hit emptied of all the coins I'd put in. Near enough a ton I'd put in there. Cunt.

JAKE Okay. Sorry... Your life is way more complicated than Cardew's.

TRUDGE *turns again.*

TRUDGE Second point. I am not unemployed. I am MC Kernow – rapper and grime artist. I am rapcore to the core me.

JAKE Yeah. Sure. I mean I see Jay-Z and Eminem inviting you to go on a world tour. Last time you rapped was up Bodmin Football Club and the committee politely asked you to vacate the stage after two songs. I know. I was there, apologising fur all the chaos.

TRUDGE They got no taste up there. They didn't get my freestylin' at all. All they wanted was Status Quo. Fucking gimpy muppets . They dun't knaw class when they hear ut.

JAKE You might be rapcore mate, but actually you're an unemployed suspended ceiling installer, who got laid off last summer on account of the economic downturn.

TRUDGE Shoot my dream dead Jake... You're following yours. I'm following mine. (*Beat*). Eh – You did say fifty quid fur the day didn't you?

JAKE Alright MC Kernow, let's get started. I'm goin' to go through the desk items and notebook here.

TRUDGE What do you want me to do?

JAKE Go through the library. See if you can find any ancient texts – anything that looks a bit different. I don't think there's much of an order or catalogue or anything. Looks like it was just placed on the shelves when it was purchased. Cardew must've known something was here though.

TRUDGE *sizes up the job and then starts on the bookcase.*

A pause.

TRUDGE Where was a from? Cornish wuz a, or from up the line?

JAKE From St Columb. His father was a Methodist minister: John Joseph Cardew. A dairy farmer before he turned to the ministry.

TRUDGE (*genially*) Eh? Do you remember that time we got 'eaved out of Sunday School Youth Club?

JAKE *shakes his head.*

JAKE Course. How could I forget.

TRUDGE Old minister – Reverend Vigus wudn' ut? – didn't like me playin' CDs inside the chapel.

JAKE Yeah – y'know why.

TRUDGE I couldn't help if the awnly discs I had was Iron Maiden's *The Number of the Beast* and Black Sabbath *Volume 4*.

JAKE Ee was probably hopin' you'd break into a Sankey session, or *Hymns Ancient and Modern*. Not crank out riffs ov the devil.

TRUDGE He'n wish on. Didn' 'appen then an' tidn' goin' t'appen now. Fuckin' Methodists fur ee.

JAKE (*talking over* TRUDGE) Cardew felt the same you know. Brought up a Methodist, but in his twenties ee converted to Catholicism. Must've made fur a bit ov tension between ee and his father. So it's said, he went over to Brittany. Saw the parish close at Guimiliau and that wuz it. He wrote about it – the church stands on an old sacred enclosure from the Age of the Saints. According to Cardew, that's what Cornwall should have been like. Took a wrong direction in the Reformation, and carried on goin' with John Wesley.

TRUDGE It's all the same thing anyway. Worshipping a dead Jewish carpenter.

23

JAKE Cardew didn' think so. He reckoned the loss of the link to Brittany was one reason why Cornwall stopped speaking Cornish. If we'd stayed Catholic then the language might have survived. Thaas' the general consensus.

All the while JAKE *is speaking he has his head down in* EDWARD'*s notebook. Occasionally, he types a few things into his laptop.*

TRUDGE Well, long time past now idn' ut. Dun't spect there's many who think bout tha' anymore. Only you and all the other beardie-weirdies who study Cornish. (*Beat*). Ere, this any good es ut?

TRUDGE *holds up a book for* JAKE *to see.*

JAKE What is ut? Who's it by?

TRUDGE Got a big Q on the cover. Hang on. Arthur Quiller Couch and Daphne du Maurier. (*looking towards the ceiling as he says the title in awe of it*). It's called Castle Dior.

JAKE Dior? You sure? That's a perfume mate – fur posh French women…

TRUDGE A'right. No tidn' Dior. It's *Dor*. Thaas' a place idn' ut?

JAKE Yeah – not far up the road. That novel was started by Quiller Couch and finished by du Maurier. It's all about Tristan and Iseult. Classic love triangle. It's logical that the Trevanions would have that title. Too early for Cardew but he would have approved. He liked the story of Tristan and Iseult. Wrote several papers on it for the *Journal of the Royal Institution of Cornwall*. All about the potential origin of the tale – on the south coast – by a writer who was Cornish – or knew Cornish at least.

TRUDGE You found anything yet?

JAKE Dunno. Maybe… I just have to fit all the pieces of the jigsaw together.

TRUDGE *is already bored by the quest, and sits back, shrugging his shoulders.*

TRUDGE Lot of books here. (*Beat*). Right, when's crib? I need a fag too.

JAKE A'right. Let's take a breather for ten minutes.

TRUDGE *gets up and produces a packet of tobacco and some rollies. Deftly he rolls a cigarette with one hand. He opens the door and walks out into the hallway.*

JAKE *rises more hesitantly, pressing SAVE on his laptop. On his way out he almost trips over* EDWARD'S *briefcase.*

JAKE (*to himself*) Idiot.

JAKE *pushes the briefcase under the table. He leaves the library. Lights down. As the transition occurs we hear the following sermon in Cornish, voiced by* EDWARD:

EDWARD Ima egglos a Rome owth incistya na yll den vith marnas an pab y honen gelwel warbarth cucell kemmyn a'n egglos; sow gowegnath pur ew henna, pecar dell esyn ny ow qwelas the orth lies exampyl. An kynsa cucell general a'n unyversal egglos a ve an cucell neb a rug dos warbarth in cite a Nice in Bythinia in blethen agyn arluth CCCXXV. Ny ve an pab a rome a guntellas an cucell warbarth na nyle espscop vith arall. Na, an cucell a ve somonys gans an emperour Cristian Constentyn.

[The church of Rome insists that only the Pope himself has the power to convene a general council of the church, which is a falsehood, as we can see from many examples. The first general or ecumenical council of the universal church was the council which met in Nicaea in Bithynia in the year of our Lord 325. It was not the bishop of Rome who convened the Council, nor any other bishop. No, the council was summoned by the Christian Emperor Constantine.]

Scene Three

The library, later that same evening. All is the same as in the previous scene. There is no attempt to remove JAKE'S *satchel or laptop. Dim light.* PIERS *enters, sits down and pours himself a brandy. He puts his head in his hands and vaguely looks over the materials on the desk. He sighs. The grandfather clock strikes eleven. Shortly afterwards, there is noise outside Rosenannon House. A carriage door is shut; The front door of the house is opened and closed. Tentatively, the door of the library is opened. A gentle and beautiful voice is heard singing a music-hall number. The voice is that of* CHRISTABELLE TREVANION.

CHRISTABELLE (*delicately*) Mid pleasures and palaces though we may

25

roam, Be it ever so humble, there's no place like home...

Into the room, enters a confident CHRISTABELLE *loaded down with suitcases and hat boxes.*

CHRISTABELLE Piers, is that you?

PIERS Darling – you're back... I wasn't sure if you would make it.

CHRISTABELLE *drops her case and boxes upstage centre.*

PIERS *gets up and moves to kiss her. She backs away. All he can give her is a peck on the cheek. They are not close and the distance between them is noticeable throughout the scene.*

CHRISTABELLE I did say. The run in Bath's finished now.

PIERS Tell me all about it. How was it?

CHRISTABELLE Good. (*excitedly*). We got fabulous reviews. There was a piece in the London Times. They liked my solos. The Theatre Royal was sold out. Darling, I had an absolute blast... Here's a copy of the programme for you.

CHRISTABELLE *places down a programme onto the table. She encourages* PIERS *to look at it but he chooses not to.*

CHRISTABELLE (*Beat*). Why are you in here? You never use the library. I was always the one who used to practise in here. You never used it at all.

PIERS Darling, don't you recall? A Mr Edward Cardew is staying here. He's an antiquarian. Wanted to look through the papers and books here. We've just finished supper. He'll be here for a couple of days. He's down from London. He's gone to bed now though. You'll like him I think – a most interesting chap...

CHRISTABELLE I see. And where's Mrs Couch?

PIERS She was tired. I told her to go to bed. She was most insistent about staying up but I explained that you and I could take care of things.

CHRISTABELLE I really could have done with her help.

CHRISTABELLE *indicates the quantity of cases and boxes she has.*

CHRISTABELLE I took the opportunity of being in Bath to purchase a few things. I know how you like me to look fashionable Piers – all those tiresome balls in Truro.

PIERS (*pleading*) So, will you be back for a bit now? Will my singing Cornish nightingale rest her wings for a while? Or has your splendid agent, Mr Goodyear, booked you another tour?

CHRISTABELLE I know what you'd prefer.

PIERS (*matching her rhythm*) I know that for the past two years, I have only seen you for about six months in total. You've been to Montana and California more than here at Rosenannon. The very house has been calling for you.

CHRISTABELLE (*exasperated*) What is it Piers? Is it the gossip you are afraid of? I know all about what you peers think – you marrying a performer instead of some lady of the manor. Don't you trust me? Are all actresses and singers flighty and loose?

PIERS No. Not at all. I'm not suggesting that.

CHRISTABELLE We're not, you know.

PIERS You know why I want you here.

CHRISTABELLE That again? But I thought we had talked about this last time I was down. Before Bath.

PIERS I think, my darling, it was more a case of you talking at me. Telling me what you wanted. We were down near the boathouse – don't you remember? You were about to push me in.

CHRISTABELLE Then you know what I want.

PIERS What about what I want?

CHRISTABELLE I've said one day, haven't I? Just not... yet. I'm not ready.

PIERS (*resigned*) So Rosenannon will go heirless. You know I can see that time in the future Christabelle. When there will be no-one to take over the estate. It will be sold to strangers. (*Beat*). Besides, I know that tone in your voice.

CHRISTABELLE (*defensively*) What do you mean?

PIERS I know it. He's asked you hasn't he? Come on Christabelle, be honest with me for once. I don't need a song or a music-hall number. I need the truth. What's Goodyear signed you up for next?

27

CHRISTABELLE Alright. But if I tell you, you mustn't shout…

PIERS I'm hardly likely to – remember, we have a guest staying.

CHRISTABELLE I've been offered a tour of South Africa. Good money, Piers. Enough to set us up for life. All the big cities: Johannesburg. Cape Town, Kimberley…

PIERS You would have everything you need here. Fowey Consuls is doing well enough – there'd be nothing you'd want for.

CHRISTABELLE But there would be… You know that isn't enough for me. You've known that ever since we married. I need to perform, to travel, to live beyond this stupid peninsula set into the Atlantic. I need to reach out past the mould and mildew of Cornwall.

PIERS (*interrupting her*) South Africa, you say?

CHRISTABELLE Yes – the place is filled with Cornish miners. I'll go down a storm. Just like I did in the States. It'll be Carson City all over again. Imagine…

PIERS Not sure I like the sound of it. There's conflict out there. The Boer Republics. They're brutal. They're not having any of it. Do you really want to step into that cauldron of fire?

CHRISTABELLE I'll be safe enough. (*Beat*). Even safer if you came with me.

PIERS I can't. I need to be here.

CHRISTABELLE The Consuls can look after itself. (*moving closer to* PIERS). Think of the experiences we would have together.

PIERS *breaks from her and strides across the room to the fireplace.*

PIERS Why does your generation of women have to prove themselves in this way?

CHRISTABELLE *reaches for the brandy decanter and pours herself a glass. She drinks a measure quickly.*

CHRISTABELLE (*between mouthfuls*) Why does your generation of men seem to think we cannot improve ourselves? Or even act for ourselves?

PIERS You always know best.

CHRISTABELLE You always think you do. (*Beat*). Anyway, what is this

28

pathetic Mr Cardew finding here? He must be an absolute bore to find anything exciting at Rosenannon?

PIERS I wouldn't say so. He's not really begun yet. You must see. He'll be here in the morning.

CHRISTABELLE I'm sure he will discover the truth pretty soon – and be gone from here as soon as he can.

PIERS In truth, he seems rather fascinated with the place, if I am honest.

CHRISTABELLE More fool him.

PIERS Don't be like that darling.

CHRISTABELLE Like what?

PIERS Hard – and tough as moorland granite. It doesn't suit you.

CHRISTABELLE I'm not sure you know me anymore Piers. I'm not the coy girl you married.

PIERS Maybe. But I think I still know you. Deep down there's still you… It's what I have always believed in, what I have always loved.

CHRISTABELLE Sometimes I feel…

PIERS Feel what?

CHRISTABELLE Like…

PIERS (*impatiently*) Like? Come, come, girl… I'm waiting.

CHRISTABELLE Stop snapping at me Piers!

PIERS Me, snappy?

CHRISTABELLE I think you'll find you're the snappy one.

PIERS (*carelessly and condescendingly*) Whatever you say, dear…

CHRISTABELLE *sighs and runs her hand over the bookshelf.*

CHRISTABELLE You should throw away all these books… (*condescendingly*) dear. None of them are ever read. I would be surprised if any of them were ever opened up anyway. I probably know it all in here better than you anyway. Don't you remember – when I used to practise singing in here?

PIERS Of course I do.

CHRISTABELLE Books aren't the way forward for this new century. Mark my words – there'll be other ways for people to be entertained. In Bath, there are stereopticons and photodramas. They are all the rage.

PIERS I know... But at least books hold messages from the past within them. Like time capsules. Just because things are old it doesn't stop them from being relevant. You should know that. Half the songs you sing are in your repertoire for sentimental reasons.

CHRISTABELLE That is because people are in love – and when they are in love, they become stupid and sentimental.

PIERS That's the reason I behave like I do then.

CHRISTABELLE It must be.

A pause.

PIERS Shall I help you with your things? I'll carry them upstairs to our room.

CHRISTABELLE Just the cases – that's all. The boxes can stay in here. I'm too tired to sort them out now.

PIERS Very well.

A discernable physical change comes over CHRISTABELLE.

CHRISTABELLE You're a good man Piers.

PIERS Really? Sometimes it seems like I am not.

CHRISTABELLE You are. But you married a butterfly who flits from flower to flower. Hear me and all my sermons about what you should and should not do. I don't mean it. I just...

PIERS ...want a different kind of life than your mother and grand-mother?

CHRISTABELLE See, you *do* understand.

CHRISTABELLE *kisses* PIERS. PIERS *moves to pick up the cases and opens the door to the hallway.*

PIERS I'll be waiting for you.

CHRISTABELLE I'll be there soon. There's a couple of things I need to do.

CHRISTABELLE goes over to one of the boxes. She unties the ribbon around it, and looks inside. She pulls out a new hat, and positions it on her head. She poses with it, then places it back in the box. Above her she notices the Trevanion Coat of Arms. She sniffs and tries to ignore it.

She moves downstage to the table and sets EDWARD'*s notebook and the* Bibliotheca Cornubiensis. *Lets her hand rest on the top of the laptop screen. She sings a music-hall number softly to herself – almost as if a lullaby.*

CHRISTABELLE   I'm neither modest, pure or shy
I sometimes rather wonder why
The censor ever lets me by
For I admit, I'm a… Bad, bad, bad, bad, woman,
but I'm good, good company.

Antiquarian? I know what he's after.

CHRISTABELLE goes over to the bookcase and taps the spine of a non-descript book.

CHRISTABELLE Don't worry my bewdie. I'll keep ee safe and sound.

She then quickly exits the library, shutting the door behind her. As the transition occurs we hear the following sermon in Cornish, voiced by EDWARD:

EDWARD Egglos Rom a lever hy the vois an vn egglos, rag, kepar dell vgons ow leverel, hy re be bythquath onen, sans ha catholyk po vniversal. Hen ew gowegnath. Ith esa yn fenogh in ystory an egglos a Rome pabe hag antypab, rag exampyl hypolytus, Novacian, an secund Constenten, Bonyfatyus, Johan, Gregory ha lias huny erel. Pan ve Urbanus deposiis ha Clement dewysys in y rom eff, res ve thyn pontyff deposys removya the Avignon in soth a Frink. Kemerys oll warbarth yth esa dew babe dre moy agys pymp cans blethan. Fatell yll an Romans rag henna leverel fatell o aga egglos y onen bythquath?

[The church of Rome tells us it is the only church for it, they say, has always been one, holy and catholic or universal. This is a falsehood. Many times in the history of the church of Rome there have been a pope and anti-pope, for example Hippolytus, Novatian, Constantine the second, Boniface, John, Gregory and many others. When Urban was deposed and Clement elected in his place, the deposed pontiff had to remove to Avignon in the south of France. Altogether there were two Popes for more than 500 years. How can the Romans say that their church was always one?]

Scene Four

Lights up on the library. TRUDGE *enters. He yawns. His eyes fall on the boxes which were deposited upstage centre in the previous scene. All other items remain on the table. He comes to stand in the middle of the room and scratches his crotch. He seems to look uncomfortable. He moves his hand inside his trousers and adjusts his meat and two veg. Smiles to himself.*

TRUDGE Ah thaas' better. Friggin' crotch-rot. (*absent-mindedly*) Boxes? Didn't nawtice they there before. This place is just full of crap. So much stuff everywhere. (*laughs*). It d'need one of they OCD types in here from Channel 4. Obsessive Compulsive Cleaners. That'ud sort ut out.

Intrigued, TRUDGE *goes over to the boxes, and opens two of them. There is nothing inside but tissue paper. He frowns, then tosses the first box into the pile. He still has hold of the second box.*

TRUDGE (*to himself*) Empty... You ent goin' t'find yer fortune in here Trudge. Tidn' naw Cash in the Attic fur certain. (*A pause*). Whaas' this say? (*peering more closely at a label on the second box*) Madam Christabelle Trevanion...

As he speaks, his mobile phone rings. The absurd phone jingle is based on 'Daydream Believer' by The Monkees. He nearly has to check every pocket before he finds the phone in his rear trouser pocket. He looks to see who the incoming call is from, then places the phone to his ear. The voice at the end of the phone speaks.

TRUDGE (*loudly*) You get my text?

TRUDGE *paces as he talks. We guess the voice to be* JAKE.

TRUDGE Where you to?

He listens to the response.

TRUDGE What ee doin' down there?

TRUDGE *listens again.*

TRUDGE Na. Na. I ebm found anything else.

He listens longer this time, nodding at the same time.

32

TRUDGE A'right, but when will you be back? If you'm gettin' pasties make mine the Super-steak one, will ee? An' get us a can too will ee?

A pause.

TRUDGE Na. Diet.

TRUDGE Right. Cheers an gone. (*Beat*). Cunt. Never listens to me.

TRUDGE *puts his phone back into his rear trouser pocket. He heads over to the table, and picks up* Bibliotheca Cornubiensis. *He flicks through a few of the pages but sees nothing of interest. Then on the table he notices the Bath Theatre Royal Programme for Christabelle Trevanion's performance. He picks it up and reads.*

TRUDGE (*to himself*) Whaas this? (*grandly – as if announcing it*) The Theatre Royal Bath Winter Season 1900-1901 presents the "Cornish Nightingale", Madame Christabelle Trevanion. The Western Wanderer with the wondrous voice. Directly returning from her tour in the United States of America to Great Britain. Accompanied by the Theatre Royal Bath Orchestra, conducted by Peter Morrison Esquire…

As TRUDGE *is reading, a breathless* ALISON HEARD *enters, carrying a wad of dusty newspapers. She places them onto the table. As the newspapers are dropped,* TRUDGE *stops reading. He looks at her and smiles. The newspaper pile remains where it has been dropped in succeeding scenes.*

ALISON I thought Mr Rowe might want to look through these…

TRUDGE Mr Rowe? Who? Oh. Jake…

ALISON Yes – ah – Jake.

TRUDGE Papers?

ALISON Yes – the family kept them – or someone from the house. Obviously when stories featured Rosenannon, they were held onto. There are more but I felt these were the most relevant – from the 1900 to 1902 period. The architect and I were looking downstairs and I remembered them.

TRUDGE Bang on then. When our man Cardew wuz here.

ALISON You could start your 'research' by going through them perhaps? Anyway, where's Jake?

TRUDGE Aw. Ee's popped out a minute. Gone t'fetch we some dinner fer a minute.

ALISON Gone into Fo-wey?

TRUDGE *looks at her twice and then the audience as he reacts to her pronunciation of Fowey.*

TRUDGE (*mimicking her*) Fo-wey I d'reckon – or Par maybe… I dun't knaw.

ALISON But you're getting on okay – in general?

TRUDGE Es. Splendid.

A pause. ALISON *moves from one foot to the other.*

ALISON Good. Glad to hear it. What was that you were reading when I came in?

TRUDGE That. Aw. Nawthin' much. Somethun' about a Madame Christabelle Trevanion performing at the Theatre Royal in Bath…

ALISON Oh yes. Now, I've heard of that. Supposedly, she had quite a voice.

TRUDGE Famous then?

ALISON Oh yes – undoubtedly. She was quite a lady from what I know of her.

TRUDGE The X Factor of her days wuz she? A proper little Leona Lewis.

ALISON Quite.

TRUDGE The boxes over there: I think they belonged to her too. There's a label with her name on it. Did she have money to burn on hats and gowns? It's what it looks like.

ALISON Yes. Now, I think I already know a little bit about her. She was the wife of Piers Trevanion, the great-great uncle of the present Trevanions who sold Rosenannon to the Trust. From what I gather, theirs wasn't a happy marriage. Seems to be a case of her career taking precedence over her time back here with him. That's what the family say anyway. Mutterings of some kind of scandal too, I believe. I couldn't get any further than that though. Needs a little bit of detective work by someone.

TRUDGE (*thinking it through*) Was this all when Jake's boy was here then?

ALISON Well, must have been I suppose. I mean, as you know, his story's interesting enough… Look. I just thought some ends might tie up there. Sorry about the state of them. They were kept down in one of the sculleries of all places. Even if the family didn't read it – I expect the staff did.

TRUDGE Jake'll be pleased. He loves all this. Right up his street.

ALISON (*giggling*) No nearer to those stupid Sermons though are you?

TRUDGE No. But something'll turn up – I'm sure…

TRUDGE *turns over the next page of the programme. He notices a picture.*

TRUDGE This here?

ALISON Who?

TRUDGE Tha' Christa-belle or whatever she was called.

TRUDGE *shows her.*

ALISON Nice portrait. Specially done for her programmes by the look of it. Quite a looker, wasn't she?

TRUDGE *moves the picture forward to refocus on it. He then rotates it to get a better look.*

ALISON What do you reckon? Attractive isn't she?

TRUDGE (*not giving anything away*) Hard to tell… It's old. ALISON's *mobile phone buzzes.*

ALISON Sorry… I'm following a couple of threads at the moment.

ALISON *holds up the screen of her i-Phone and using her forefinger scrolls down through several stories.* TRUDGE *watches her movements.*

TRUDGE Anything good?

ALISON Just people joking about the referendum. Usual kind of thing.

A pause.

TRUDGE So, Alison, gotta ask – did you vote then?

ALISON (*surprised at* TRUDGE's *directness*) Sorry?

TRUDGE For the Assembly? Did you vote for the Assembly or not like?

ALISON No. Well, yes. I did vote. But I didn't vote for the Assembly. I mean, I think we're better off in the Union really. Always have done. Cornwall's too small to go it alone. I don't really think we're enough of a national minority. I know that's probably not what you think... but...

TRUDGE I see. You Cornish?

ALISON Yes – I've traced the family back several generations. We were around Mylor in the 1640s I believe. My aunt did some research.

TRUDGE But?

ALISON But what?

TRUDGE (*smiling*) You didn't feel the need to... you know... put your X in the right place like?

ALISON People's politics are probably best left out of conversations like this. Especially at the moment. It's not like I'm unpatriotic.

TRUDGE No. Course. I understand. (*Beat*). Each to his an' her own an' tha'...

ALISON I take it that you voted – for. I get that feeling from you.

TRUDGE Really? Well, actually, m'andsome, I cudn' be bothered.

ALISON (*exasperated*) Couldn't be bothered? I don't believe you.

TRUDGE Well, twas like this. I wuz goin' to – and then well, we had a bit ov a sess up the Boscawen: a late one and then a lock in – and tha' resulted in a full-on all-nighter back Nanpean – few wraps of speed, out with the old Metallica albums – so in the end I had a bit of a kip. Woke up and thought I should, but then I cudn' be assed. Woke up again, and twas all over.

ALISON So you left the fate of things to others?

TRUDGE Sometimes I find thaas' the best way. You'n blame others then. Not yerself. Thaas' the way I d'look at ut.

ALISON It looks like the YES vote has won anyway.

TRUDGE A surprise to me tha', considerin' all the emmets who voted. All them tools with second homes down St Mawes and Fowey an' the like who think they'n tell we party what to do.

ALISON Is that really what it's like? What you think?

TRUDGE It's what your man Cardew here thought. Ee saw the writin' on the wall didn' a? I mean, I knaw ee didn't get t'see the like o whaas' appened t'places like Padstow, and the rest ov the 45,000 new houses we d'need to make up fur the 45,000 owned by they up the line… But yeah, fur me an' Jake, thaas' what tis like.

ALISON Cardew?! Was he really the first to suggest Home Rule here?

TRUDGE Es. According to Jakey-boy twas a crucial aim of Cowethas Kelto-Kernewek.

ALISON Who were they?

TRUDGE A cultural preservation group. Same period. Bet they buggers are turnin' in their graves eh?

ALISON Someone has to I suppose. *(Beat)*. Look I'd love to chat some more… but I'd better be getting back… I only came here to…

TRUDGE Well, I'd better get on with goin' through them papers. See gin.

ALISON *moves to make her way out of the door, then looks back on* TRUDGE. *She smiles to herself.* TRUDGE *is plucking up courage to ask her out, but before he can speak, the door has closed.*

TRUDGE *(trying and failing to be cool)* Alison, are ee doing anything later? If not, perhaps you'd like to come up Nanpean fur a bite to eat?

TRUDGE *notices she has gone.*

TRUDGE Ah shit. Thaas' blown tha'. Twudn' never work anyway. Now she d'knaw I'm a fuckin' Cornish fundamentalist and she's well, like Victoria fuckin' Beckham.

TRUDGE *puts his head in his hands, then looks down at the programme.*

TRUDGE Christabelle. You'd go out with me wudn' you? A good Cornish maid like yerself.

While TRUDGE *is talking to the picture,* JAKE *walks in.*

JAKE *(partly to himself an partly to the audience)* WTF?

TRUDGE Wha'?

JAKE I go out fur half-an-hour, an' you've lost it.

37

TRUDGE Lost what?

JAKE Any sense you still had? You there, talkin' t'that picture. (*Beat*). There y'go – Super-steak an' a can of diet just like you asked fur.

JAKE *passes him a large pasty and can of diet coke.*

JAKE Ah Christ. I know tha' face.

TRUDGE What face?

JAKE You asked her out haven't you? I knew it y'knob. You've probably blown the whole thing.

TRUDGE No.

JAKE We'd better eat ut outside – not in here… Library rules.

TRUDGE (*steering the conversation in a more favourable direction*) So – did you do what you needed to do?

JAKE (*whispering*) What – the photocopying?

TRUDGE Yes? All done?

JAKE Got ut sorted – yeah. Dun't tell her. Makes it easier in the long term.

TRUDGE Good. (*Beat*). Did you see Alison?

JAKE Yeah – briefly. Looked like she wuz in a hurry. (*Beat*) Why are we whispering?

TRUDGE (*whispering*). Dun't knaw. (*louder*). I mean, I dun't knaw.

A pause, while JAKE *unpacks his pasty and opens a can of Tango.*

JAKE So?

TRUDGE So what?

JAKE So – find anything did ee?

JAKE *gestures for them to leave the library.*

TRUDGE (*mouth already deep in his pasty*) I told you before. Nah – nothing. Not really anyway. There's nothun' ere.

JAKE *and* TRUDGE *leave the library, both drinking their cans of drinks and eating their pasties. The lights fade down. As the transition occurs we hear the following sermon in Cornish, voiced by* EDWARD:

EDWARD I lever egglos Rome fatell ve hy sans pub termyn. Gow molethys ew henna ha lavar a'n Jowl. A dus tha, ny alla ve in termyn cot alowys thym rag an progath ma expowndia thewgh oll an cammensoth a mar lias pab. An nawves Benedyct, rag exampyl, a ve pab teyrgweyth rag prys cut hag eff a werthas y office deweyth ha cafus mona ragtha. Aswonys da ve avell sodomita. Johan pab, an pymthegves a'n hanow na a ladras rychyth an egglos in rom hay ranna in mysk y woos nessa. An tryssa Sergius a rug moldra an pab a theth theragtha y honen ha wosa bos gwris pab eff a rulyas an egglos gans an gweras a horys. An trethegves Johan a rug chy horys a balys Laterano ha eff a wre defollya benenas pilgrim. Eff a ve lethys gans gour y gowethes gwely. Innocentyus an peswora a'n hanow na a vsyas tormentys rag examnya herytyckys. An wheffas Alexander a rug conquerrya oll Italy dre weras y vab y honen, ha eff a gemeras y virgh y honyn avell cowethes gwely. Kyn whrug numbyr bras a'n pabow ledya bewnans an moyha fyltya, ny vanna ve leverall tra vith moy rag an present termyn ma, rag me a grese nag ewa honest evyn the wull mencyon an taklow ma the orth an purcat.

[The church of Rome tells us that she has always been holy. This is an accursed lie and an utterance of Satan. My dear people, I cannot in the short time I have for this sermon, expound to you the wickedness of so many popes. Benedict the Ninth, for example, was pope for three short periods, and twice he sold his office for money. He was well known as a sodomite. John XV stole the wealth of the church in Rome and distributed it among his relatives. Sergius III murdered his predecessor and when he became pope ruled the church with the help of whores. John XIII turned the Lateran palace into a brothel and raped women pilgrims. He was killed by the husband of his mistress. Pope Innocent IV used torture to interrogate heretics. Pope Alexander VI conquered Italy with the aid of his son, and took his own daughter as concubine. Although very many of the popes led lives of unutterable depravity, I will be silent about any more of them now, for it is not seemly even to mention such things from the pulpit.]

Scene Five

The lights come up on the library. EDWARD *is busily at work, leafing through volumes he has taken off the bookshelves. He is so involved in his work, that he barely notices* CHRISTABELLE *enter the room. She stands for a while, watching* EDWARD. *She is not quite fully dressed, and has entered the room wearing only a dressing gown and a slip. Eventually she speaks.*

CHRISTABELLE You must be Mr Cardew?

EDWARD Yes – delighted to meet you. You must be Chistabelle. Piers told me much about you at supper last night.

CHRISTABELLE All good I hope.

EDWARD Most certainly.

CHRISTABELLE I'm afraid I only arrived at Rosenannon late last night – so needed to sleep in this morning. I missed breakfasting with the pair of you.

EDWARD Not a problem my dear. He is devoted to you. He has told me about your stunning singing and music-hall career. He says you may well be off to South Africa very soon? Is that right?

CHRISTABELLE If it comes off, yes – then I hope to go there.

EDWARD You will know South Africa is, in parts, more Cornish than Redruth or Camborne.

CHRISTABELLE So I have heard.

EDWARD They will greet you like an angel, I know it.

CHRISTABELLE But Mr Cardew, you have not heard me sing yet.

EDWARD Perhaps that may be remedied during my stay. I do hope so. I grew up with music you see – my father being a Methodist minister. It is in the blood, so to speak.

CHRISTABELLE For me too. It engulfs me. Piers doesn't feel it like I do – but then how could he? He is more mining and shipping than melody and song…

EDWARD He says the two of you are planning a family.

CHRISTABELLE (*surprised*) Did he now?

EDWARD (*embarrassed*) I meant not to intrude.

40

CHRISTABELLE No – no intrusion. It is true. We do plan a family – but sometime in the future I think.

EDWARD He would prefer now?

CHRISTABELLE Your intuition serves you right Mr Cardew. He would prefer it to be sooner, but I have other things to do in my life before motherhood. (*Beat*). Are you married Mr Cardew?

EDWARD I am.

CHRISTABELLE And do you have any children?

EDWARD Alas no. We have not been blessed in that way. Besides, I think it best we have not. I would not make much of a father. My books and manuscripts – well, they are like children to me. Some are well-behaved and others are not – but they are each precious in their own way.

CHRISTABELLE I see. A career-minded soul. Just like me. (*under her breath*) How I crave that sometimes...

A pause.

CHRISTABELLE Has Piers shown you where everything is?

EDWARD Well, as helpful as he can be. My task now is to go through the collection and see what is here. Boase and Courtney – as he probably explained to you – they are pointing towards an interesting manuscript.

CHRISTABELLE I see. And dear Mrs Couch. Has she kept you fed and watered?

EDWARD Wonderfully. Tea every hour if I want it – alongside copious supplies of biscuits. She really is a dear.

CHRISTABELLE I know. We were fortunate in finding her. (*Beat*). What precisely is it that you seek at Rosenannon?

EDWARD Hopefully. a book of wonders. I am interested in the old Cornish language Mrs Trevanion. And at Rosenannon perhaps is to be found a manuscript from 1680 with a set of Sermons inside it – both in Cornish and in English. It is this that I seek.

CHRISTABELLE How incredible.

EDWARD Well, it is when you think what these things have had to survive and endure. We are perhaps lucky that anything has survived. The modern world sometimes does not value antiquity.

CHRISTABELLE What would this manuscript look like?

EDWARD I don't know to be honest. It could be large or quite small. No-one ever knows. *Ordinalia* – one of the manuscripts we have – is actually quite small. I always hope for something larger... More spectacular somehow...

CHRISTABELLE Is it bound?

EDWARD Well, I suspect it might be. Manuscripts really, but in truth, if it were a few scraps of paper I would be happy.

CHRISTABELLE How do you think it got here?

EDWARD Piers asked me the same thing. Who knows? The Trevanions once had properties in the West – where these Sermons were preached – so maybe they were inherited or compiled from a distant source. (*Beat*). Do you know the library, Mrs Trevanion?

A pause.

CHRISTABELLE No. I'm afraid I do not know it very well at all. It's always been one of those rooms I didn't explore much – and these days, I don't have a lot of time when I come back...

EDWARD I started over there – in the left-hand corner. All sorts of things there you know. Some Stannary regulations and land charters. Lots of Cornish field names – which I have noted, but nothing much more as yet. The heart must remain hopeful, however.

CHRISTABELLE Of course. (*flirtatiously*). The heart must always be such.

EDWARD *and* CHRISTABELLE *exchange a glance. Embarrassed,* EDWARD *returns to his notes.* CHRISTABELLE *smiles to herself, and goes over to the boxes. She pulls out the same hat she took out the previous night, and places it on her head. For a while, she stands there, waiting for* EDWARD *to comment.*

CHRISTABELLE What do you think?

EDWARD The hat?

CHRISTABELLE Yes.

EDWARD Splendid. It suits you, Mrs Trevanion.

CHRISTABELLE I got it in Bath – at a shop just across from Sydney Gardens.

EDWARD For the tour?

CHRISTABELLE What?

EDWARD For the tour of South Africa?

CHRISTABELLE Oh, yes – perhaps.

EDWARD Or maybe a walk around the streets of Fowey? In either case, if I may say, it sets you off well. (*Beat*). Bath's interesting.

CHRISTABELLE Why?

EDWARD Oh well, it fell to the West Saxons in 577 after the Battle of Deorham... close by. After that, well, I suppose the inevitable was going to happen...

CHRISTABELLE Go on?

EDWARD Well, that the language would retreat down the peninsula. Back to Exeter – and then thanks to Athelstan – back to the Tamar, and then thanks to just about everything else into Penwith and into oblivion.

CHRISTABELLE I know that's sad – and so on, but have you ever thought that sometimes oblivion must be wonderful. Oblivion. Such a beautiful word. Even more beautiful when you put it with into. Into Oblivion. That, Mr Cardew, is sometimes how I want to be: 'into oblivion'.

EDWARD I understand I think... We humans sometimes need to leave our mark – but sometimes we prefer oblivion – as you put it.

CHRISTABELLE *still has her hat on. She comes over to sit on the table next to* EDWARD, *displaying her legs to him.* EDWARD *is at first not distracted but by her silence is forced to notice her.*

CHRISTABELLE Tell me Mr Cardew, in that Cornish, was it always the same over time or did it change and move like English? Because well, I sing lots of songs in my set that have older English words in it, and I wondered the same about this Cornish.

EDWARD A fascinating question. Actually, Cornish altered quite a lot over time. As you might expect, some words and concepts stay the same, but others mutate and change over time. Some observers believe Cornish was purest during the medieval period, but that's nonsense. The language was just as vibrant towards the end of its life...

CHRISTABELLE But hadn't it been corrupted?

EDWARD Corrupted? How do you mean?

CHRISTABELLE I mean by English. Surely more English words start appearing in it...

EDWARD I see. Well, when you put it like that – then perhaps so. But then again, languages never stay the same. They are always evolving. For some it may be corruption; for others it is pure Darwinism.

CHRISTABELLE Evolving. That's another word I like. Evolving. It's got a nice sound to it.

EDWARD Perhaps so...

CHRISTABELLE Evolving into oblivion. That's me, that is.

EDWARD Now, why would you want to do that?

CHRISTABELLE I don't know. A woman's prerogative I suppose. (*with child-like enthusiasm*) Tell me, are there any songs in Cornish? I should like to learn some if I can. I am a Cornish singer. I ought to know a song or two in Cornish.

EDWARD You really want a song in Cornish?

CHRISTABELLE Yes – if there are some... or maybe you could write one for me?

EDWARD The latter is impossible. My Cornish is not yet good enough but let me think – yes, there is a song I know... I have the lyrics of it in my notebook.

EDWARD *hastily fetches his notebook.*

EDWARD Come, look. Here's how you say it.

EDWARD *reads out the words to* CHRISTABELLE.

EDWARD (*slowly*) *Pelea era why moaz, moz, fettow teag,*
        Gen agaz bedgeth gwin, ha agaz blew mellyn?

CHRISTABELLE (*hesitantly*)
Pe ... lea era why moaz, moz, fett ... ow teag,
Gen agaz bed ... geth gwin, ha agaz blew mel... lyn?

EDWARD That's it. You're a natural...

CHRISTABELLE *smiles at* EDWARD.

EDWARD Here's more...
Mi a moaz tha'n venton, sarra wheag
Rag delkiow sevi gwra muzi teag.

CHRISTABELLE (*with more confidence*) Mi a moaz tha'n venton, sarra wheag, (*then with satisfaction*) Rag delkiow sevi gwra muzi teag.

EDWARD Perfect. Absolutely perfect. You speak...

CHRISTABELLE (*interrupting*) What?

EDWARD (*in awe*) You speak the language so naturally...

That translates to
Where are you going pretty fair maid,
With your white face and your yellow hair?
I'm going to the well, sweet sir,
For strawberry leaves make maids fair.

CHRISTABELLE nods her understanding.

EDWARD Alright. Here's the second verse:

(*slowly*) *Pea ve moaz gen a why, moz, fettow teag,*
Gen agaz bedgeth gwin, ha agaz blew mellyn?
Greuh mena why, sarra wheag,
Rag delkiow sevi gwra muzi teag.

This means
Shall I go with you pretty fair maid,
With your white face and your yellow hair?
Do what you want, sweet sir,
For strawberry leaves make maids fair.

Here's the tune.

EDWARD *gives her the tune and improvises the first couple of lines from the song.*

EDWARD It's called 'Strawberry Leaves' and was written by Edward

45

Chirgwin in 1698. Probably just a translation of an English folk-song but no matter. Will you try singing it?

CHRISTABELLE *sings the song, tentatively yet with great beauty.*

CHRISTABELLE   *Pelea era why moaz, moz, fettow teag,*
Gen agaz bedgeth gwin, ha agaz blew mellyn?
Mi a moaz tha'n venton, sarra wheag,
Rag delkiow sevi gwra muzi teag.

Pea ve moaz gen a why, moz, fettow teag,
Gen agaz bedgeth gwin, ha agaz blew mellyn?
Greuh mena why, sarra wheag,
Rag delkiow sevi gwra muzi teag.

EDWARD That was wonderful. It is the first time I have heard the piece sung.

CHRISTABELLE It's amazing. I will practise.

EDWARD (*smiling*) There does seems to be a synchronicity between us Mrs Trevanon, doesn't there?

CHRISTABELLE There does. It's not something I notice very often.

CHRISTABELLE *becomes physically closer to* EDWARD *here.*

EDWARD We are like souls I believe.

CHRISTABELLE Are there other verses?

EDWARD Yes – I will teach them to you. I'll write down the lyrics.

A pause. EDWARD *goes back to his notes.* CHRISTABELLE *hums and sings bits of the song. Eventually she stops and comes around to the front of the table to make eye contact with him.*

CHRISTABELLE Is the book you're looking for called *The Sherwood Sermons*, Mr Cardew?

EDWARD (*distractedly*) Yes – did Piers tell you?

CHRISTABELLE No. I worked it out myself.

EDWARD Well, yes. That's it. The Sherwood Sermons. By Reverend Joseph Sherwood. From 1680 in fact. Only eighteen years after Chirgwin's song.

CHRISTABELLE Nothing to do with Sherwood Forest then? Or Robin Hood?

EDWARD No. Nothing to do with that.

CHRISTABELLE (*flirtatiously*) Shall I let you into a secret?

EDWARD *now looks up.*

EDWARD What kind of secret?

CHRISTABELLE One that you will want to know.

EDWARD Really? I sometimes find secrets are not good things. Honesty and openness are better.

CHRISTABELLE Alright. Well, if I'll tell you though you must promise not to let anyone else know that I found it.

EDWARD Mrs Trevanion – you are talking in riddles.

CHRISTABELLE Maybe – but do you promise?

EDWARD Promise.

CHRISTABELLE Our secret – between you and I.

EDWARD *rolls his eyes and goes back to his note-taking.* CHRISTABELLE *skips, like a girl, over to the bookshelf and locates a brown leather-covered book. She comes back to where* EDWARD *is sat and stands behind him. There is something sensual and seductive about her closeness to him.*

CHRISTABELLE Close your eyes.

EDWARD *closes his eyes.*

EDWARD These games are a bit tiresome, Mrs Trevanion. Come, I have only a limited time to work here.

CHRISTABELLE Well, when you open them, you won't have to search any more.

CHRISTABELLE *nuzzles into* EDWARD'*s neck and shoulder. He continues looking straight forward, but with his eyes closed.*

CHRISTABELLE (*seductively*) Give me your hand.

EDWARD *turns over his hand, and she plops the book into it.*

CHRISTABELLE Open your eyes.

EDWARD *looks down at his hand.*

CHRISTABELLE Our secret, yes?

EDWARD What is it?

CHRISTABELLE What does your heart tell you it is?

EDWARD (*in disbelief*) No?!

CHRISTABELLE What does your heart want it to be?

EDWARD I know what I want it to be.

CHRISTABELLE Sometimes, Mr Cardew, you just have to have a little faith.

EDWARD Are these what I think they are?

CHRISTABELLE They are. Only book in here called *The Sherwood Sermons.* Look for yourself.

EDWARD *feels the cover and then turns to the title page, where the title of the volume is confirmed.*

EDWARD You found it?

CHRISTABELLE I never lost it. I've always known where it was. Just didn't know it was anything important – that's all. I didn't know what the weird writing was on the left-hand side of each page. I thought it was just someone messing around. Now I know what it is. See, there's about fifty of them.

EDWARD I must go through and translate – take notes. What a find! Boase and Courtney were right.

Joyous, EDWARD *stands. Involuntarily, he wraps his arms around* CHRISTABELLE, *who does not resist his attentions. As if by magnetic attraction, the two kiss, both consumed by utter wonder. The kiss becomes a bit more than a celebration of the discovery. It lasts a little too long. However,* EDWARD *becomes the first to break away.*

EDWARD I'm sorry. I didn't mean to… The joy of the manuscript… This is of national significance… You realise that? It…

CHRISTABELLE …made for a bit of oblivion?

EDWARD Well, er, you might say that.

CHRISTABELLE I didn't find it oblivious Mr Cardew. I thought we evolved a little bit then...

EDWARD Maybe we did.

The door opens and in walks PIERS. CHRISTABELLE *adjusts her clothing.*

PIERS Any joy?

EDWARD Well, actually Piers, Christabelle here has just helped me locate what might be it...

PIERS By Jove! You mean you've found it?

CHRISTABELLE Well, I didn't exactly. Mr Cardew was describing the manuscript and I recollected something like it. Not that I know much about this place.

PIERS Is that it?

EDWARD Yes – see...

PIERS Well I never. *The Sherwood Sermons.* There it is in black and white. What do they say?

EDWARD I don't know. I haven't got that far.

PIERS At least you've found the things you came for. I was afraid it would be like hunting for a needle in a haystack. I'm dashed thirsty anyway – been down for a meeting with the quarry captains this morning – but this calls for the best tea and china. I'll call Mrs Couch...

EDWARD (*to* CHRISTABELLE) Thank you.

CHRISTABELLE Not at all.

EDWARD No – really. I have you to thank.

CHRISTABELLE I'll go – and let you and Piers have your moment of discovery.

EDWARD What will you do?

CHRISTABELLE What I always do. Sing. I'll go and practice 'Strawberry Leaves'. You carry on...

CHRISTABELLE picks up the notebook and leaves EDWARD *on his own, as he begins devouring the first sermon. A look of utter abandonment falls across his face, as he rapturously reads the text. The lights fade down. As the transition occurs we hear the following sermon in Cornish, voiced by* EDWARD:

EDWARD An pabow hag escobow egglos Rom a berthy own pub termyn pan ve treylys an scriptures sans the davas an bobill henna the removya the worth an prontyrryan han epscobow an otham anothans the expowndya blonogath Dew the'n bobill crystian. Lacka whath dyr redya an scriptures in aga eyth aga honyn an bobyll cristian a vynsa gwelas pana bell ew comondmentys Crist ha'y awayl the orth lewd bewnans an pabow, an epscobow ha'n mebyon lien erel. Rag henna an egglos Roman a rug oll aga ehan pub termyn the lettya treylyans an scriptures the eyth an bobill. Pan rug an prontyr sans Johan Wicliff in reign an secund mytern Richard gorra in mes y dreylyans an beybel in eyth an Sawson an egglos an abusyas in moyha vyl termys ha prysonys ve gansans. Warlerth y virnans an egglos a Rom a'n declaryas the vose eretyk. Y gorff a ve palys in ban ha leskys.

[The Popes' and Bishops' church of Rome have always feared that the holy scriptures translated into the language of the people would remove the necessity of the priests and bishops to expound the will of God to Christian people. Worse still, by reading the scriptures in their own tongue, Christian people would see how far are the commandments of Christ and his gospel from the wicked lives of the popes, bishops and other clergy. The Roman church therefore did all they could to stop the translation of the bible into languages understood by the people. When the godly priest John Wycliff in the reign of the second king Richard completed his translation of the first bible in English he was viciously abused by the church and imprisoned. After his death the church of Rome declared him a heretic. His body was dug up and burnt.]

Act Two

Scene Six

The library, as before. By the brightly-lit feel of the room, and by the time on the grandfather clock, it is clearly the second day of JAKE*'s research at Rosenannon.* JAKE *is sat at the table upstage centre, while* TRUDGE *moves around the room.* TRUDGE *is now more relaxed in the room, and through the course of the scene, he sits and relaxes on most pieces of furniture, though positioning his body at unconventional angles. He is quite literally treating it as if he is on the television programme, 'Big Brother'.*

TRUDGE *(in a Geordie accent)* Day Two in the 'Big Brother' House and Jake Rowe is studying the incredible life of Edward Cardew, language guru, Celtic Revivalist and hero of the People's Republic of Kernow. *(looks up to see if Jake is taking any notice)* And late last night, the boy Trudge shared an intimate moment with pop diva Nicole Scherzinger in the swimming pool. Couldn't possibly give you the detail on ut because it might shock ya, but let's just say it involved rampant sex until the small hours. OK magazine's doing a feature on ut.

JAKE *stops working and looks up.*

JAKE What are you doing?

TRUDGE Just trying to entertain you. You look bored.

JAKE I'm not bored. I'm content. I'm working my way through everything.

TRUDGE I know, but are you finding anything out?

JAKE Course I am. The papers – they report that Christabelle Trevanion and Piers Trevanion become estranged from each other in the time after 1901. They never seem to get divorced though – but it feels like she never comes back to Rosenannon.

51

TRUDGE Whoopee do. But what's that got to do with our man Cardew?

JAKE Well, he was here for a few days when she came back from Bath. We know that.

TRUDGE *moves so that his head is upside-down. He simulates sex as he says the next line.*

TRUDGE (*joking*) What – so he shagged her did a?

JAKE Cardew?

TRUDGE Yes.

JAKE No. He'd never have done that. I mean he'd been married for ten years before. All the notes indicate they were happy.

TRUDGE Who was his wife then?

JAKE Emma-Leigh Pollard. She was a ball of energy too by most people's reckoning. Helped Cardew a lot. Trained as an artist at Slade, but then turned her hand to poetry, and helped teach the language – like her husband. Catholic too. From an old Cornish family – descended from the Arundells.

TRUDGE But there's nothing on her here is there?

JAKE No. Nothing. Why would there be?

TRUDGE *moves to the table and picks up the programme containing the image of* CHRISTABELLE.

TRUDGE Just wondered. Just wondered if in his notes he was thinking about her the same way I think about Nicole Scherzinger. I mean if he was pining for her, then he ent likely to be having any on the side down here is a? But on the other hand, this Christabelle's a bit of an enigma ent she? Might have gone fur a bit ov glamour among the bookends.

JAKE What under the nose of Piers – his host?

TRUDGE Why not? Been done before edn ut?

JAKE Only in your world Trudge. Na – I cen't see it. Dead end I d'reckon. It's got t'be the manuscript that changed him – that made him do what he did.

TRUDGE Sometimes you don't make any sense t'all. What – you saying that Cardew found somethun' he didn't like and because of tha' he freaked out?

JAKE I dunno. Maybe. There are two questions really. One – why isn't the book still here? We can't find ut anywhere. Second – why did he appear to rip out all his notes from the time here? Look – see, where the pages are all gone.

TRUDGE That's what you copied wasn't it? The book with all the tears in it.

JAKE Yes. It's crucial somehow.

TRUDGE This *Handbook* you keep going on about?

JAKE What about ut?

TRUDGE What – so he'd almost finished it by the time he came to Rosenannon? He was just hoping to find out something else to put in it.

JAKE Seems that way. I mean the *Handbook* was more or less finished. David Nutt, his publishers, were ready to go on it, but there's a letter I found in the RIC archive where obviously Cardew has asked them to hold fire for a while. He thinks he may have found something else.

TRUDGE Weird. *(Beat and changing tone)*. So pard, wasson with we two tonight? Never mind this lot, what's the weekend got in store? I d'reckon we owe ourselves a good bit of 'r n r'.

JAKE *(quietly)* Dunnaw.

TRUDGE Dunnaw? What ee mean, you dunnaw…

JAKE I just dunnaw. Maybe I want to work some more on this.

TRUDGE Oh, hang on. Hang on. Hang on. I know the way you said, dunnaw then. I know that kind of tonal attribution. Dunnaw there means 'Get lost Trudge, coz I got a shag in the bag'. Thaass' zactly what that kind of dunnaw means. So MC Kernow loses out again…

JAKE MC Kernow get himself enough action anyway dun't a?

TRUDGE Do a? It dun't feel that way. Last time I had any was New Years' Eve, with Mona Juleff's niece. That wuz hardly what you call the most passionate moment ov my life. It all happened because ov me using the blow torch on the Chinese lanterns that I got from Trago.

JAKE Dun't go there… Besides, you do a'right.

TRUDGE Prob'ly do d'a'right fur an unemployed suspended ceiling installer. But you, like this. Na. There's summin' on. I can tell. (*Beat*). Got it. I got ut. She's asked you out ent she?

JAKE Who?

TRUDGE Miss Green Welly. Whatsername: Alison…

JAKE You wuz the one who liked her… All that posing by the fireplace remember?

TRUDGE Yeah – but I could tell twas a losing battle. I knawed it wuz you she wuz interested in. So come on, spill the beans? She has, hasn't she? Earlier today – yeah – when I went fur a fag down near the lake – and you and she wuz talkin'…

JAKE Alright. She kind of asked me out. Said she was thinking of going' down Sam's – you know, over Polkerris. Bite to eat an' that.

TRUDGE You lucky, lucky bastard. So you snapped her hand off?

JAKE No.

TRUDGE (*incredulously*) No?

A pause, while TRUDGE *processes this information.*

TRUDGE Are you insane?

JAKE Maybe.

TRUDGE I just dun't get you. Ever since we wuz at school, all the best maids ask you out, and you fuckin' blaw it every time. I mean…

JAKE You mean wha'?

TRUDGE (*quietly*) Dunno. Just don't get it. Thaas all. If twas me, I'd be walkin' over broken glass t'go out with her. Not very often a boy from up St Dennis gets an offer like tha'.

A pause.

JAKE (*assuredly*) You know why.

TRUDGE Do I?

JAKE Yeah – course you do. You've known it fur a while Trudge. You just dun't want to speak about ut – thaas all.

TRUDGE I thought…

JAKE No. You thought wrong boy.

TRUDGE Goes back to when?

JAKE I told you. Ancient history edn' ut?

TRUDGE Goes back to chapel – that time you told me about.

JAKE *nods.*

JAKE He knew it and I knew it…

TRUDGE Yeah – but didn' mean twas right though do ut?

JAKE Look. When Reverend Vigus touched me, it felt…

A pause.

JAKE …good. So I knew then.

TRUDGE Yeah – but, well, ee was meant t'touch people in a different way – with prayer an' tha'; not a fumble backstage between scenes ov the chapel nativity. Should have been ad up for it – fuckin' Jimmy Savile he wuz.

JAKE Trudge. It weren't like tha'.

TRUDGE What wuz ut like then?

JAKE It awakened me – thaas' all. Told me who I was. (Beat). You need to know: I forgive him.

TRUDGE You kept ut quiet long enough.

JAKE Well, you do, don't you? National minority status on the streets but we've still got people gettin' their heads kicked in because they dun't fit. Goth, gay, grime, geek – it dun't matter.

TRUDGE I never judged you pard.

JAKE I know Trudge.

TRUDGE I dun't give a shit mate. You'm my mate – thaas' all tha' counts. (*Beat*). Look, fancy a walk? You haven't been down to the estuary yet have you? It's nice. Cardew went down there. Thaas' where they found un. Do ut shall us? You'n always come back to this lot later on.

TRUDGE *and* JAKE *leave through the door. As they leave, we hear* TRUDGE'S *voice.*

TRUDGE So – with this Alison then, I might still be in with a shout?

As the transition occurs we hear the following sermon in Cornish, voiced by EDWARD:

EDWARD Johan Hus o pronter sans in Bohem neb a garsa glanhe in mes a'n egglos oll an practys lewd ha camhensek o tevys inhy. Eff a ve prysonys gans an papistys saw delyvrys ve wosa henna ha promys a ve res thotha gans emperour Almayn Sigismundus; an kymyas a ve ris thotha may halla eff travla dhe gucel Constans ha egery thothans y thesyre pur the wul thyn egglos dewhelas the sansolath corff Crist. An emperour bytegyns a dorras y solem ly avell Cristion. Huss a ve sesys, prysonys arta, tryys avell heretyk, ha leskys yn few.

[Jan Huss was a saintly priest of Bohemia who wished to cleanse the church of all the wicked and pagan practices that had arisen in her. Huss was at first imprisoned by the papists but released and given a promise of safe conduct by the German emperor Sigmund; this was so that he could travel to the council of Constance to explain his pure desire to return the church to the godliness of Christ's body. The emperor broke his Christian oath. Huss was arrested, imprisoned again, tried as a heretic and burnt alive.]

Scene Seven

Morning. The library. The door opens and ANGELA *and* EDWARD *enter.* ANGELA *is fussing over* EDWARD, *who appears to have aged overnight. He walks shakily and uneasily. She holds his elbow to steady him.*

ANGELA You sure you'm a'right my 'andsome... You looked some flustered over breakfast... A bit peaky if I might say so.

EDWARD (*trying to recover*) I'm fine, thank you. Really. It's just that I couldn't sleep last night... what with all the excitement of the discovery.

ANGELA By the sounds of it, you wuz working away.

EDWARD You heard?

ANGELA I don't miss much in this house. Couldn't sleep though, you say? Wuz ee warm enough? Wuz the bedding not comfy fur ee?

56

EDWARD It was all fine Mrs Couch. More than fine. It was this dratted book that kept me up, rather than any problem with the bed or room...

ANGELA That book. You mean the one you found, my lover? I'm some glad you found ov un though. Be some terrible if you had a wasted trip here an' that.

ANGELA escorts him to the table, and finds him a seat there. EDWARD sits.

EDWARD Well, yes. I had to get on and translate it. You see, the Sermons are in Cornish and English, but then there's the question of whether the translations match.

ANGELA pauses to think about this.

ANGELA So, do they then?

While they speak, ANGELA checks the fire and puts another log on.

EDWARD Well, yes... They do. Not much licence on behalf of the translator...

ANGELA How do you mean?

EDWARD Well, sometimes when a text is translated, the translator puts a certain spin on it: their mark so to speak.

ANGELA Caw d'hell. I never knawed that. Not they then?

EDWARD No. Not at all. The two texts are like parallel lines.

ANGELA Whaas' ut say then? *(jokingly)*. I mean, es ut a good read?

A pause.

EDWARD *(guardedly)* Well, I can't really say yet... I have more checks to do on it. One must not leap to conclusions in such matters. I must double-check things this morning...

ANGELA Sermons wudn' um? All religious an' tha', es ut? Moast of they kind are idn um?

EDWARD *(trying to hide his true feelings)* You could say that.

ANGELA Well, I'll tell ee what my lover, I'll leave ee t'get on my 'andsome. The last thing you want is someone like me pussivantin' round ee. Now, cup taa and biscuits the normal time?

EDWARD *turns and smiles at* ANGELA.

EDWARD That would be splendid, Mrs Couch – ah, Angela...

ANGELA Right you are Mr... Edward.

ANGELA leaves. As soon as she goes, EDWARD *begins to busy himself with the processes of enquiry. He uses his magnifying glass.*

EDWARD Blasted woman... At last, a bit of peace and quiet... to think... what to do...

EDWARD *goes back to* The Sherwood Sermons. *He stands at a distance from the book, almost afraid of it. He circles it, never letting his gaze move away from it. The impression we should get is that the book is dangerous and powerful.*

EDWARD *(to himself)* Corrupted. I never thought in a million years... And you've lain here all this time... and me, the idiot, has to find you – and all that you conjure...

During these speeches, EDWARD *stares forward, alienating the audience.*

EDWARD *(disturbingly, as if in a trance)* Get a grip. Come on. You've read worse haven't you? You've read worse. Must check. Must check the meaning again.

Gingerly, EDWARD *sits and steadies himself. He opens the book and reads to himself. He opens his notebook and checks his translation. He grimaces and shakes his head, not enjoying what he is reading. He almost beats himself up about what he is seeing. He pounds his fists into his head.*

EDWARD No... No... But it can't be. It can't say that. How the hell can it ever say that? How is that the truth? How on earth does Sherwood think that? He's a fool... a braggart... a liar... I must counteract it – find more texts. I know there are more out there. I know it. Then I'll show Sherwood... show him what it's about. Show what a sham he is.

With the aggression of a bear, EDWARD *finally loses self-control, and throws* The Sherwood Sermons *across the room. The book lands somewhere upstage right.*

EDWARD *(shouting)* Bleddy thing...! Get out of my sight!

EDWARD *leans forward onto the table, pushing his hands through his hair in frustration and anger.*

EDWARD (*in almost physical pain*) Your words will maim... I cannot let you out... You would harm our chances of nationhood... of being a minority... I will not circulate what you have to say...

Then once more, the book attracts him again. First his one eye, then the other, falls upon the book on the floor upstage right. He stares at it for a while.

EDWARD (*directly addressing the book*) You dare insult me in my language, eh?

EDWARD *stands up and moves to where the book is lying on the floor. He sighs. He bends to pick it up, almost faltering as his hand touches the cover. Then, he confidently holds it up in the air, examining it in the light. As he is doing this, the door of the library opens and in walks* CHRISTABELLE. *She watches him and listens.*

EDWARD (*to himself*) Books – they shouldn't scare people. But you...

CHRISTABELLE No. They shouldn't. What about it?

CHRISTABELLE'*s voice unnerves* EDWARD *and he drops the book to the floor.*

CHRISTABELLE You had better be careful with that. It's old, you know. Priceless. I know an antiquarian who'd like a look at it. (*Beat*). You look terrible...

EDWARD I feel terrible.

CHRISTABELLE I didn't sleep either. Been thinking. Went for a walk in the grounds at two o'clock. In the sunken garden. I saw your light on.

EDWARD (*breathlessly*) I've been reading. Translating. Checking. The Sermons – you wouldn't believe it.

CHRISTABELLE Tell me about them then? What do they say?

EDWARD (*downbeat*) They say everything I don't want them to. They're beautiful works of art but... there's a wall of separation...

CHRISTABELLE A wall of separation?

EDWARD *stands up.*

EDWARD I mean I never thought I'd ever find a manuscript that appalled me – that made me have to rethink and re-evaluate everything. The Cornish in them is incredible – new words and concepts, as well as forms confirming all I had ever thought – but their message – what they say, makes me sick to the very core.

CHRISTABELLE You can't alter that. It is a risk you take in your line of work.

CHRISTABELLE *stands close to him.*

EDWARD I never thought it would come to that. I never thought I would open such hatred, such deep incisions into my own self.

CHRISTABELLE You and Sherwood I take it – at opposite ends of the spectrum?

EDWARD Well, yes. He's Protestant – and I'm…

CHRISTABELLE …a newly-constructed Catholic?

EDWARD It was another Age. Shifts in belief happen. I accept that. It happened in me. But it's not just that – Not just the way he demolishes the Virgin Mary (although that's harsh enough) – but the other concepts – they go completely against the grain.

CHRISTABELLE What do you mean?

EDWARD All of it – everything I believed in… Although some of the main tenets he argues for – all according to God's will of course – is that the Cornish should give up on the language. It is dying he argues, and they'd be better off embracing English. Life would be easier then, he argues. Then there's a long treatise on the Grail. Joseph of Arimathea never brought it back to Britain – it thus renders the Arthurian material as pure mythos – utter fiction – with no meaning…

CHRISTABELLE Surely legends do not have to be real to carry meaning though? I mean we know this from our childhood. The truth is in the story alone.

EDWARD (*speedily*) Not in this way. He demolishes all meaning. Likewise – you know I told you I contributed that chapter to the book on *Fairy Faith* for Dr Evans-Wentz – Sherwood detests such ideals. According to him the imagination of fairies, and brownies, and *bucca du*, piskies, spriggans and knockers – they are all the work of the devil, impinging on the work of the Christ… But you see, I – me – Edward Cardew – have such belief in them. So many stories about them I have collected over the years – I cannot just dismiss them they way he has. But there it is – written in the finest Cornish.

CHRISTABELLE Just because you disagree with the argument doesn't mean the Cornish is invalid, surely?

EDWARD I have a responsibility.

CHRISTABELLE To whom?

EDWARD To the future. To the nation. Such arguments can be seen. The Cornish have already had their backs broken by failing mines and emigration. Now this. Can I really put this before the public? Is it really in our interest? There's more – look... (EDWARD *flicks through the pages*). He dismisses Cornwall's separateness. Says we were never that distinct. Never different. He embraces the reign of Charles II, and that it is good that Cornwall is now fully merged into England. Don't you see?

CHRISTABELLE I see that this text contradicts your arguments. But are you the one to censor it? Should you play God and tell people what to read and what not to?

EDWARD (*angrily*) With this, I see why censorship can be good. I see now why it is needed.

CHRISTABELLE I'd never have believed you would say that.

EDWARD Things change. Here, look... Sermon 14 praises the work of King Athelstan... and yet, we know he did terrible things to speakers of the language. He told the "filthy Cornish" to leave the city walls of Exeter... For Sherwood, he is a hero, a man to be admired. See...

CHRISTABELLE But obviously he still saw the importance of writing in Cornish... He still had parishioners who needed to hear what he said in Cornish and not English.

EDWARD Did he? Maybe he was coerced. Forced to translate – and only that. Perhaps he saw the bitter irony of what he was doing. And here. This, I agonised over. No matter how I translate it, it tells of dispute between the Bretons and the Cornish. The Cornish at this time hated the way the Bretons came over and took their jobs and women... This was not the way things should be. They used to be brothers in arms: Brythonic partners.

CHRISTABELLE Should be, or are? Edward, you are shirking from real history. If you don't accept these exist then you are in denial. History is fluid, competitive and full of discourse. It is not set in stone. Would you have it intractable – only the history that you prefer?

EDWARD No... I know. It goes against everything my mind tells me, but the heart – it tells me something different.

CHRISTABELLE Would you prefer not to have discovered them? You came here – to Rosenannon – to seek them? And I helped you... I suspect it wouldn't have mattered if I hadn't shown them to you. Eventually you would have found them.

EDWARD Why? Did you ever think of not showing them to me? Of hiding them?

A pause.

CHRISTABELLE Perhaps. Yes – perhaps I did. I had no idea what they contained. I couldn't read the Cornish and the English was hard enough for me to understand. But they somehow belonged to me... I was the only one who'd ever looked over them – I mean, before you.

EDWARD And you'd have stopped me from viewing them?

CHRISTABELLE If I had known how they would have broken your heart, then yes. If I had known they were a Pandora's Box, then yes, I wish you had never opened them.

EDWARD Knowledge cannot be undone. Once it is there, it is there forever.

CHRISTABELLE Edward, this is one voice. Maybe it is a mad voice. A voice of someone who doesn't know the truth the way you do. Conceive of it as that, and you may find peace.

EDWARD But the words... they cannot transcend Rosenannon. They will cause all I have worked for to topple like a game of dominoes. We have enemies you see. There are those who want us to be uniform, who mock our difference, and mock our claims. This will be grist to their mill.

CHRISTABELLE You have no idea of the future. From what Piers has told me, your work has already been accepted and is well-respected.

EDWARD But this has authority... antiquity... I am a Johnny-come-Lately.

A pause.

CHRISTABELLE You, Edward, are afraid of ghosts.

EDWARD Rather I think I know how certain spectres behave.

EDWARD *looks directly at* CHRISTABELLE.

CHRISTABELLE Listen to me. Sometimes we may not like what the past has to say. We must accept it though – remembering it is really not the present or the future. *(Beat)*. How can this one little book have such power?

EDWARD Books are powerful. You know that. Think of the Bible. Just the same way the songs you sing are powerful. They ignite in us deep passion; they fire us to the very core.

CHRISTABELLE Is that why you think it has remained hidden? A kind of disease best not talked about?

EDWARD I don't know. It could have ended up with any family – not just the Trevanions...

CHRISTABELLE Well, the Trevanions have a terrible cancer inside of them. You know that... It's a kind of restrictive, self-destructive part of their biology.

EDWARD A biology all the Cornish have in my view.

A pause.

CHRISTABELLE What are you going to do?

EDWARD I cannot unlearn what I have learnt. I will have to take this to my grave.

CHRISTABELLE Isn't it better to know this now, rather than if you had come across it after you had finished your *Handbook*?

EDWARD The *Handbook* will be a sham now. I cannot tell the full story...

CHRISTABELLE You still can Edward.

EDWARD This arrow comes deep from the past. It is poisoned-tipped. It has turned to dust everything I have believed in.

CHRISTABELLE No. Not everything. You are stronger... I know it.

EDWARD Am I? I feel broken. My joints have been ripped from their sockets.

EDWARD collapses onto the floor in despair. CHRISTABELLE sits on one of the chairs.

CHRISTABELLE All is not lost really. Your hope will transpire into something good – I know it... Come, lie your head down here and rest.

CHRISTABELLE *points to her lap.* EDWARD *looks at her. It is as if he is a child.*

CHRISTABELLE Here...

EDWARD *moves his head onto her lap. The move is both sensual and loving.* CHRISTABELLE *strokes his head, and hair. She moves to unbutton his tie. He resists her desire to do this.*

CHRISTABELLE There. You see. Sherwood cannot touch you – or harm you. I shall make sure of it.

EDWARD *already realises their position is problematical.*

EDWARD We... But Piers...

CHRISTABELLE Piers went early this morning. He shan't be back.

EDWARD *breathes heavily.*

CHRISTABELLE Try to calm yourself. (*Beat*). Besides, you already know I am not interested in Piers....

EDWARD *breathes more slowly.*

CHRISTABELLE I mean, I was surprised... when you took an interest in me...

A pause.

EDWARD Who are you interested in?

CHRISTABELLE Come – I do not need to answer that. Both of us were lost. Lost souls on the edge of life. Now we have found each other.

CHRISTABELLE *turns her head from him.*

A pause.

EDWARD *trembles.*

EDWARD Last night, I touched myself – in bed – thinking of you... Made myself hard... wishing for your presence.

CHRISTABELLE stands, shocked at his directness.

EDWARD I'm sorry. So very sorry. I shouldn't have said that. It's just that...

CHRISTABELLE Go on...

EDWARD Mrs Cardew and I, we don't – and you... such passion... such wonder... so desirable. I could not help it.

CHRISTABELLE You don't make love?

EDWARD No. I have never seen her body.

CHRISTABELLE (*laughs*) Never?

EDWARD *shakes his head and looks to the floor.*

CHRISTABELLE Make love with me...

> CHRISTABELLE *grabs him tightly and kisses him erotically. They fumble at each other's bodies, unstoppably passionate.*

CHRISTABELLE Come –write new words with me Edward.

> *They undo each other's clothing.*

CHRISTABELLE Speak to me – in Cornish... Tell me all that you feel...

EDWARD *Ahanas je yth hunrojaf dre'n nos. Yma y'm colon gwir whans growed-ha genes.*

CHRISTABELLE That's it.

> *Their entwining is erotic, powerful and all-consuming, far from the tension witnessed earlier on in the scene. The pair fall onto the table, scatting the materials and objects we know from previous scenes in the play.*

EDWARD (*breathless and passionate*) Sing to me... 'Strawberry Leaves'... please...

CHRISTABELLE (*erotically*) *Pelea era why moaz, moz, fettow, teag,*
> > *Gen agaz bedgeth gwin, ha agaz blew mellyn?*
> > (*between kisses*) That song. It's saucy...

EDWARD I know.

CHRISTABELLE Don't stop.

EDWARD I won't.

More clothing is undone as the two become even closer. Just at the moment where we think their passion is unstoppable, EDWARD *breaks away from her, gasping.*

CHRISTABELLE No. No. What are you doing?

EDWARD *(gasping)* I can't. I mean I mustn't.

CHRISTABELLE Why not?

EDWARD I'm married. You're married. I don't do this kind of thing.

CHRISTABELLE But you are… You wanted to.

EDWARD I may have wanted to but I need to restrain myself.

CHRISTABELLE What? Like you were in bed last night – awake and a-thinking of me.

EDWARD No. I need to curb my behaviour. I have made vows. You made vows.

CHRISTABELLE This isn't 1680, Edward. This is a new century. We are consenting. We can do what we like.

EDWARD We can't.

CHRISTABELLE Who says?

EDWARD My faith.

CHRISTABELLE Your faith now, eh? Your will is stronger than that faith of yours. You know it.

EDWARD His faith then.

CHRISTABELLE Whose?

EDWARD Joseph Sherwood's. His.

CHRISTABELLE But you hate what he says.

EDWARD I do. He's wrong on just about everything. But in Sermon 21 – he's right…

EDWARD *picks up the book to find it. He shoves it towards* CHRISTABELLE'*s face. She takes the book from him.*

EDWARD Read it.

CHRISTABELLE reads it. EDWARD paces, doing up his shirt, and tidying his appearance.

EDWARD What's it say?

CHRISTABELLE It's all about how Cornishmen should not covet the wives of others... whther they be ladies of the manor or fish jowsters or balmaidens. How they must resist temptation... That's what you are doing right now, is it Edward?

EDWARD Yes. I have come to my senses.

CHRISTABELLE What, returning to your loveless marriage? And me, to mine?

EDWARD It would be better that way.

CHRISTABELLE No. I can't believe you. I don't believe you. One minute, this Sherwood is your worst enemy. Now he's your best friend. The Sermons are pure evil you say, and yet this small piece is now utterly moral and correct.

Exasperated, EDWARD doesn't know what to say. He breathes heavily, desperately trying to find logic and understanding.

CHRISTABELLE I thought you were different, Edward. When I met you, I thought, there is a man whom I could love. Not this arranged agreement I have with Piers. You – a real man. But now, you show me you are just as much of a sham as he is. And I am to be shamed and vilified.

EDWARD *(as a whisper)* Not vilified... No... Nor shamed.

CHRISTABELLE Be brave then...

EDWARD All my life I have tried to be brave. Why should I be any different now? I was brave, Mrs Trevanion, when I shook off the shackles of Methodism – and had my family ex-communicate me... I was brave when I suggested Cornwall could be a Celtic nation again. I was brave when I suggested Home Rule. *(Beat)*. Today, I shall be brave again.

Slowly and deliberately, with his right hand, EDWARD takes The Sherwood Sermons from CHRISTABELLE. At first, she will not release them, but then relents. As if beaten and bruised, EDWARD takes one last look at the book. He smells the paper, and traces the lettering with his forefinger.

EDWARD (*to himself*) Beautiful. Exquisite...

Then, decidedly and with utter confidence, he takes the Sherwood Sermons over to the fireplace. He bends and places the book onto the fire. To his right, CHRISTABELLE *gently weeps. We hear the roar of the fire and the sound of the book igniting.*

EDWARD There. Now it is done.

CHRISTABELLE *continues to weep.* EDWARD *crosses the room behind her.*

CHRISTABELLE Change history would you? You don't have that power!

EDWARD *halts.*

EDWARD Sometimes, we have that power.

CHRISTABELLE (*angrily*) Feel better for it, do you?!

EDWARD *pauses to think. He looks up.*

EDWARD I only feel guilt – unstoppable and unrelenting.

CHRISTABELLE Good – you deserve it.

EDWARD Cursed. That is me now. I am cursed with guilt.

EDWARD *leaves.* CHRISTABELLE *sits on a chair and places her head into her hands. She sobs, and with waves of emotion crumples. The lights go down. As the transition occurs we hear the following sermon in Cornish, voiced by* EDWARD:

EDWARD Martinus Luther pronter ha broder a ordyr Austyn in mysk y lies ober arall a ros dhe bobill Germany treylyans a testament coith ha'n testament nowith in aga eyth aga honyn. An papisticall party a rug judgia an lyfrow na hag a levery aga bose cam in lies forth ha fatell esans ow containya mer a false discas. Nyna an papistical pronter Ierom Emser a gemeras treylyans Luther, y chaungya very nebas omma hag ena y publyssya in dan y hanow y honyn avell version compas an egglos roman catholyk the chalyngia treylyans Luther. Mar te nebonyn ha redya treylyans Emser ha treylyans Luther warbarth, apert ew warlergh termyn cut an thew lever the vose an kethsam treylyans. Theworth hemma, a dus tha, ny a yll desky dew dra: kynsa fatell rug an papistical party falslych acusya Luther a heresy, ha secund fatell russans leveral gow then bobill kristyon pan leverens nag esa valew vith in y dreylyans.

[Martin Luther, priest and Augustinian friar, among many other godly works gave the German people the old and new testaments in their own language. The papists immediately condemned his translation and said it was mistaken and contained much false teaching. The papist Jerome Emser, however, took Luther's translation, altered it very slightly here and there and published the work under his own name as the Roman church's correct version to rival Luther's. It is apparent from a cursory reading that Emser's bible and Luther's bible are the same book. From this, good people, we learn two things: first, that the papists falsely accused Luther of heresy and second, that they lied to the faithful when they said his German bible was of no value.]

Scene Eight

ALISON *enters the library.* JAKE *and* TRUDGE *are nowhere to be seen. She investigates the materials on the table and* JAKE's *laptop. She is on her mobile phone.*

ALISON (*breezily*) Hi Polly... It's Ally... Yeah, yeah, still at work... No, over Rosenannon. On the old estate... Yes – do come over and have a look sometime... (*listens*). Tonight? Not sure if I can do tonight. Sounds absolutely lovely though. (*listens*). What's that?... Oh, the scholar and his monkey. Well, monkey-boy had the hots for me. How embarrassing! Soon pissed on his fireworks though... Yeah, the other one? I tried asking him out. (*listens*). You'd like him. Rugged. Bit rough-looking. (*laughs*). Something about him though. Cute with it. (*listens*). Not sure he's interested. Said he couldn't. Gave him such a lead on though... (*laughs*). Perhaps he'll reconsider. (*listens*) Yeah – right then. Let me sort something out. On my way. Ciao.

ALISON *presses the stop call button on her mobile.*

ALISON (*to herself*) Bitch.

ALISON *looks at her phone and finds another number. She presses the call button and waits for a response.*

ALISON (*loudly*) Hiiiii – David. It's Alison. You at work still? (*listens*). Look, about tonight. Something's come up here. (*listens*). Yes – I know, I know. I know... I do still want to come to Stein's with you but you know how the Trust is... They expect you to work through thick and thin. (*listens*). Mmmmm... yes... the tower... The weather's had such an effect on it... (*listens*). Okay... Okay... You're a love – you really are. Okay. Big kisses. Mmmm... Bye...

ALISON presses the stop call button on her mobile.

ALISON (*to herself, and with venom*) Bastard. Serves him right.

As she is saying this, TRUDGE enters the library.

TRUDGE A'right?

ALISON Fine. Perfectly fine.

TRUDGE Someone you dun't like?

ALISON (*haughtily*) You could say that.

TRUDGE There's plenty about.

ALISON Aren't there just.

TRUDGE You don't mind me a –

TRUDGE begins to sort through the newspapers.

ALISON No. Course not. You carry on.

A pause.

TRUDGE I d'reckon you've got ambitions.

This working-class directness of TRUDGE unnerves ALISON. She shifts from foot to foot.

ALISON Ambitions?

TRUDGE Yes – you know... You're more Waitrose than Asda...

ALISON looks puzzled but laughs.

TRUDGE A bit more Sainsbury's than Aldi...

ALISON laughs again.

ALISON (*warming slightly*) Maybe... And you?

TRUDGE Most of my ambitions have already been met.

The conversation here should be very awkward.

ALISON Really?

TRUDGE Well, when I was at school, I wanted to be a rapper...

ALISON But?

TRUDGE And I became one.

ALISON Right.

TRUDGE When I'm doin' ceilings... (*rethinks*) when I *did* ceilings... then I'd make up rhymes and beats all the time.

ALISON That's good.

TRUDGE Yes – it wuz good. But then you get older. You're older and you don't want to do it as much. People... they...

ALISON *gestures for* TRUDGE *to speak.*

TRUDGE ...they don't listen as much. You're there but you're not there if you know what I mean.

ALISON (*honestly and with understanding*) I do.

A pause. ALISON *and* TRUDGE *think about what has been said.*

TRUDGE Nice place this, idn ut? Rosenannon.

ALISON Yes.

TRUDGE Some lot of history here an tha'?

The conversation here suddenly becomes more fluid.

ALISON These places always have ghosts.

TRUDGE People in the past still here I suppose.

ALISON (*breathlessly*) Layers of time...

TRUDGE ...stacked on one another.

ALISON Like Lego.

TRUDGE Yes – like Lego.

ALISON *moves to leave.*

ALISON I must – a – go.

TRUDGE Eh – if tha' David idn't treatun' you right, you tell me eh?

ALISON *reassesses* TRUDGE.

ALISON I will.

71

ALISON *leaves.*

TRUDGE *shakes his head and makes a little air mix gesture with his hand. He sits down at the table and puts his head in his hands. As he dozes, have* EDWARD *walk into the library.* TRUDGE *does not notice him. At this point there is a genuine blending of the time periods of the play.* EDWARD *moves over to the desk and ignores the presence of* TRUDGE. *He picks up his magnifying glass and leaves. As the door closes,* TRUDGE *is disturbed from his doze and does a double-take at the door, thinking that he has heard someone leave. He shakes his head, unconvinced he had heard anything at all. He goes back to his doze. The lights go down. As the transition occurs, we hear the following sermon in Cornish, voiced by* EDWARD:

EDWARD An egglos Roman catholik a levar nag es kymyas gans an pron-tyrryan kemeras benenas in maryag, saw ima aga practys ow contra-dia an rule ma: ima an egglos catholyk ow regardya prontyrryan a egglos an grickys avell gwyre brontyryan hag ith ew prontyrryan grek alowys dhe themethy hag in gwir ima an rann vrassa anothans ow temethy. Ha pelha ith o tus maries lies onyn a pabow an auncyent egglos. Pedyr y honyn neb ew gilwys gansans an kensa pab o demethys, rag ny a red yn awayl (Matt. 8.14) fatell rug agyn arluth yaghe an vam a wreg Pedyr

[The Roman church says that priests may not marry, but their prac-tice contradicts this rule, for the Catholic church accepts as true priests the clergy of the Greek church and the Greek priests are allowed to marry and most do in fact marry. Moreover many of the earliest popes were married men. Peter, whom the papists call the first pope, was himself married, for we read in the gospel that our Lord healed Peter's mother-in-law (Matt. 8.14).]

Scene Nine

The library. Early morning. EDWARD *is at the table. Apparently controlled and entirely sure of what he is doing, we see him tear out pages of his notebook and stuff the pages into his jacket pockets. He then places the notebook back down on the desk.* PIERS *enters and notices him at work.*

PIERS Up to much, old boy?

EDWARD Oh no. Just tidying up. Sorting out some of my notes.

PIERS (*energetically*) Ah yes. So, are you done with your researches now? Back to London is it?

EDWARD I thought I might go this afternoon – if that is good with you. There's a train at twenty past two.

PIERS Absolutely fine. But do spend a few more days here if you like. It's no matter to me. In fact, I'd welcome the company.

EDWARD No. I really must be heading back. Besides, I need to write up my findings. If I am quick, I can submit to the *Journal of Antiquities* for their autumn edition.

PIERS I see. Well, you'd know the score on that. (*Beat*). So where's the manuscript?

EDWARD Manuscript?

PIERS The Sermons?

EDWARD (*nervously*) What of it?

PIERS Will it stay here – or do you plan on carting it off somewhere – to the British Museum for example? I mean, one doesn't mind. If you need to. (*Beat*). I say, I don't see it on the table at the moment...

EDWARD It's – ah – back there on the shelf.

PIERS *turns to look back at the shelf.*

PIERS Oh – yes, of course. So, you don't think you'll need it?

EDWARD I think it best if it stays at Rosenannon. It's your heritage Piers. You should savour it.

PIERS Yes. I see. Well, of course, I look forward to seeing your article. It'll all be printed up no doubt... Much easier to read than that blasted freehand. I don't know how you do it. (*Beat*). Mr. Cardew, you seem slightly troubled. Are you alright?

EDWARD I'm fine. You know I can't help being excited by such things. They come out in a kind of nervousness in me. My wife notes it all the time.

PIERS (*conspiratorially*) Well, our wives know everything about us don't they?

EDWARD They certainly do.

PIERS (*laughing*) Between you and me, I am kept on such a tight leash sometimes…

EDWARD Oh… Where is Mrs Trevanion this morning? Is she well?

PIERS (*Beat*) Apparently not. A little moody with me this morning. One of her heads. Who the hell knows why? Women – they are as impenetrable as your manuscripts I feel.

EDWARD You may well be right. (*Beat*). I'll see her before I go though?

PIERS Oh – she's sure to come down at some point.

EDWARD Good. I wouldn't want to leave without…

PIERS Of course.

EDWARD And you, Piers? What have you to do today?

PIERS I'm out visiting some of the clay pits. There's talk of the union wishing to strike at Carthew. Damned nuisance really. Have to be there for the negotiations.

EDWARD What are the men after?

PIERS Oh you know. What they are always after. More money. Less time working. More time sitting on their asses. Still that's the future dear boy.

EDWARD I know. I'm sure you will be able to give them a better deal.

PIERS Well, one tries. One does try.

A pause.

PIERS I know you have big plans for Cornwall, Mr Cardew. Maybe you're right. Maybe we should fight a little bit harder eh? Take on these London types who bully us.

EDWARD I don't know if I have any big plans anymore, Piers. I have just made some suggestions, that's all.

PIERS Well, the more I speak to you – and learn of your ideals – the more I come around to your way of thinking. Me – speaking Cornish to the manor born. I can't see it – nor in the men of the mines… But I admire your endeavour… very much.

EDWARD Some may think me an ass – but I don't care.

PIERS Precisely the right attitude, Mr Cardew.

PIERS *notices* EDWARD *looking at the lugger again.*

PIERS You like the model?

EDWARD Very much so. It has beautiful lines. These were the kind of boats that the very last speakers of Cornish would have sailed in… William Bodinar and his crew…

PIERS Have it.

EDWARD I was not angling for that.

PIERS I know. I know. But please have it. Take it back to London with you – as a reminder of your time at Rosenannon. To me, it is just an object, but to you I see it is something more – something alive and kicking… with meaning…

EDWARD It's most kind of you.

PIERS Well, we're just about done then, eh?

EDWARD Would you mind if I went for a walk in the grounds this morning? I've been so busy I haven't really had time to explore out there.

PIERS You should. The grounds, though I say it myself, are superb – even in February. They were designed by Humphry Repton. You want to follow the sunken garden down past the lake, down through the shell grotto – to the estuary. I find a great peace down there. Such stillness.

EDWARD Is there much wildlife?

PIERS Oh yes – on the mudflats. Yes – the tide is out, so plenty of birds.

EDWARD It's where I feel I need to go. The language – it always connects one to the landscape you know. It's all about the way the past named its world. When I walk I go through the old names for the birds, the plants, the animals. It comforts me.

PIERS Well, you should find many to name down there. Take the lugger… Test it out on the lake… if you have time.

EDWARD Really?

PIERS Yes – it's a working model. My grandfather made it so.

EDWARD Do you know? I think I might.

75

EDWARD *lifts the model boat off its stand.*

EDWARD Goodbye then Piers...

PIERS Oh well, yes, goodbye. Have fun down there.

EDWARD *shakes* PIERS' *hand, then casts a longing glance into the fireplace. He eyes his materials on the table, but then turns from them. Carrying the model of the lugger, he leaves.*

PIERS *focuses his mind on objects in the room – in particular objects left from the future. He checks them for dust, or plays with them.*

PIERS Well, I'll be jiggered. Never seen that before. Never knew Father had that. Must get one of those. Looks rather handy.

Other phrases may be improvised here as the two eras meet. As he is talking to himself in this way, CHRISTABELLE *enters the library.*

CHRISTABELLE *(viciously)* I thought you were off to Carthew this morning.

PIERS I am. I was speaking to Mr Cardew... He's not long gone. He's taking a walk down to the estuary.

CHRISTABELLE I see.

There is visible tension between PIERS *and* CHRISTABELLE *which manifests in them circling each other, like trapped animals.*

PIERS *(conciliatory)* Look, darling, I've been thinking. Perhaps you are right. Perhaps I should come to South Africa with you...

CHRISTABELLE You've been thinking. have you?

PIERS *(honestly)* Yes. Intensely – over the past few days.

CHRISTABELLE *(bitterly)* Well, I've been thinking too.

PIERS What about?

CHRISTABELLE About what is to become of us. You know what I want and I know what you want – and yet, we are unable to compromise. Our histories wipe out our present or so it seems to me.

PIERS *(with hope)* Need it be that way?

CHRISTABELLE I have come to the conclusion that there is no middle way. We have become strangers to ourselves if we are honest. We have fallen into oblivion. Please, Piers, just be honest with me – this one time...

PIERS *turns towards the fireplace. He takes a poker, and pokes the flames.*

PIERS You've met someone, haven't you?

CHRISTABELLE No. How could I meet someone in this damp cave?

PIERS In Bath? London? (*Beat*). What do you mean then?

CHRISTABELLE I mean that I have realised something about us. I have realised something about how we lead our lives. How we conduct ourselves, how we interact. Somewhere in the midst of living, something has become lost. Something is now hidden that was once so open about us.

PIERS (*joking*) You sound like one of those old Sermons.

CHRISTABELLE Do I? Maybe it's because I need to.

At this, PIERS *becomes angered and strides from stage left to stage right. He points at* CHRISTABELLE *as she speaks.*

PIERS Just stop your sermonizing at me, Christabelle. I'm the one who's stood by you – allowed you this career, allowed you to travel. Please don't harp on at me. I have given you freedom beyond that which most women desire.

CHRISTABELLE But is it true freedom, Piers? Or am I still bound to you? I am still your worker – just like the men at Carthew pit with their hoses and horses.

PIERS What are you saying?

CHRISTABELLE I am saying that I would give all this up. I would give up the Trevanion name, this house, the estate, the gardens – and you, yes, you – for some real freedom. Do you know, I have seen it? I have seen it in Bath, and in California – women who are not contained or constrained by their pasts, but who lead their lives as they feel. That is what it is about. That is what I want.

PIERS I want to try to offer you that, Christabelle. Really.

CHRISTABELLE Feeling comes with passion. Passion comes with deeds and words.

PIERS I can show you that.

He moves to kiss her. Momentarily, there is a return of that passion but then CHRISTABELLE *pushes* PIERS *away.*

PIERS (*shouting*) Not like that then?

CHRISTABELLE Like that, but with…

PIERS With what?

CHRISTABELLE I don't know. I'm sorry Piers. It just seems something has died in me. I… am… broken. I have evolved.

PIERS Broken? Evolved?

CHRISTABELLE As if all I knew was certain and secure, and then something altered irrevocably.

PIERS (*now more tender*) What is that something, my nightingale? Tell me…

CHRISTABELLE I only wish I could.

PIERS But we agreed. No secrets.

CHRISTABELLE I know. But sometimes secrets are the only way. Secrets are what makes one's life tick. They touch us in ways which make us complete.

PIERS You are speaking in riddles again Christabelle. Ever since I've known you, you've been the same. When you want to talk things through with logic and sincerity, you know where I am.

CHRISTABELLE Is that your last word?

PIERS It is.

CHRISTABELLE Very well. You'll find me in my room. I'll be rehearsing.

PIERS Rehearsing? That is you all over darling. Rehearsing. Life's not a rehearsal though. It is the real thing now. I only want to live it with you.

CHRISTABELLE *leaves.*

PIERS *is left on his own. He picks up one of the hat boxes, laughs at the absurdity of his position, and throws it hard and purposefully across the room. His attention falls upon the bookshelf and the place where he believes* The Sherwood Sermons *should be located. He pulls out numerous books, and briefly scans them. When they turn out not to be* The Sherwood Sermons *he drops them like litter onto the floor. Gradually, the speed at which this is happening increases, until eventually he pulls down whole swathes of texts and runs quickly through them. When they are rejected, he tosses them to the floor.*

PIERS (*to himself*). Has to... has to be in here somewhere!

In the end, he crumples to the floor and assumes a foetal-like position. He rocks gently back and forth.

In the hallway, there is the noise of voices, fast and panicked. One of them is that of ANGELA. *These voices stop* PIERS *from rocking. Instead, he listens intently; his body tense.* ANGELA's *voice becomes clearer.*

ANGELA (*scared*) Wait there. I'd best tell Mr Trevanion. He's in the library I think.

PIERS *visibly tenses as* ANGELA *slowly opens the door.*

ANGELA Mr Trevanion? You there?

PIERS I'm here. Over here. By the bookshelf...

ANGELA Whatever's happened?

PIERS Nothing. I was just looking, that's all...

ANGELA Beg your pardon, Mr Trevanion – but I think you'd better come see. Tidn' very nice.

PIERS What is it Mrs Couch?

ANGELA The gardeners – they found this, look... on the lake.

ANGELA *produces the model of the lugger, but it is wrecked and destroyed. Its masts are bent and broken.*

ANGELA And you'd best come down to the estuary. In the water, they've found somethun'.

PIERS (*nervously*) Go on...

ANGELA Mr Cardew's body sir...

79

PIERS Cardew?

ANGELA Mmmm… Taked his own life by what they'm saying of.

PIERS *struggles to his feet.*

ANGELA Shock idn' ut? I mean, only an hour ago, I was servin' of un his breakfast… Now he be flat out down there – in the marshes.. They got a boat hook to un, I believe.

PIERS But, he seemed…

ANGELA Seemed, sir?

PIERS Seemed so calm, so sure. *(Beat).* I must go down there.

ANGELA Sir – shall I tell Mrs Trevanion? She's upstairs. I knaw she wuz very fond ov Mr Cardew…

PIERS *thinks for a moment; his hand to his chin.*

PIERS No – I'll tell her. She'll need comforting I know…

ANGELA I'll make sure of that sir.

PIERS Thank you Mrs Couch… You're such a dear.

PIERS *strides out of the library and is halfway into the hallway. At the door, the two exchange glances.*

ANGELA *(knowingly)* And the police and the papers? You knaw how gossip d'spread.

PIERS When I come back up, I'll prepare a statement.

ANGELA Very well sir.

PIERS *leaves.* ANGELA *looks over the items on the table and repositions* EDWARD*'s suitcase. From backstage, a recorded version of 'Strawberry Leaves' is heard.*

CHRISTABELLE *Pelea era why moaz, moz, fettow teag,*
Gen agaz bedgeth gwin, ha agaz blew mellyn?
Mi a moaz tha'n venton, sarra wheag,
Rag delkiow sevi gwra muzi teag.

Pea ve moaz gen a why, moz, fettow teag,
Gen agaz bedgeth gwin, ha agaz blew mellyn?

Greuh mena why, sarra wheag,
Rag delkiow sevi gwra muzi teag.

As this is heard, ANGELA *looks over at the mess of books on the floor. She shakes her head, unable to do anything about it at this moment in time. Tutting to herself, she turns off the light, and leaves. The room falls silent. As the transition occurs we hear the following sermon in Cornish, voiced by* EDWARD:

EDWARD Martinus Luther kyns oll a gowsas warbyn an pab pan esa cannas an pabe Johan Eck ow cuntell mona rag buldya egglos Pedyr in rome dre wertha indulgencys. An papisticall egglos a levery y hylly yndulgencys relesya enevow an re marow theworth punyshment in purgatory, unweyth a pe mona ris kyns thyn catholik egglos rag gweres ow buyldya egglos Pedyr in cyte. An papisticall party a lever fatell usy an power an egglos the relesya thyworth punyshment in purgatory ow springia thyworth tresour an egglos, a ve cuntellys dris an osow. Ima an tresour ma, ow concistya, in methans y, in oll an oberow da gwris gans an sens a vght an pith o res thethans. An tybyans na ew desmyk an Jowl, rag agyn Arluth y honen a lever thy dissiplis: sic et vos cum feceritis omnia quae praecepta sunt vobis dicite servi inutiles sumus quod debuimus facere fecimus (Luc. 17.10) hen ew the styrrya: 'Indella whi inweth, pan vo puptra gwris genogh a vowgh why kylmys the wull, leverogh: 'Ny ew servygy vnworthy, rag ny russyn ny gull marnas an pith a ven ny constrinys the wull.' (Luc. 7.10)'

[Martin Luther first opposed the papacy when the pope's legate Joann Eck was collecting money for building St Peter's church in Rome by selling indulgences. The papists claimed that indulgences could release the souls of the dead from punishment in purgatory, if only money was given to the Catholic church to help with the building of St Peter's church in the city. The papists claimed that the power of the church to remit punishment in purgatory derived from the treasure of the church, amassed over the years. This treasure, they say, consists in all those good works done by the saints above what was necessary for them to do. Such a notion is a devilish invention, since our Lord himself says to his disciples: sic et vos cum feceritis omnia quae praecepta sunt vobis dicite servi inutiles sumus quod debuimus facere fecimus, that is to say 'Thus you also when you have done everything you were bound to do, say: We are worthless servants, for we have done what we were obliged to do.'] (Luc. 17.10)]

Scene Ten

Lights up on the library. JAKE *and* TRUDGE *are sat at the table next to the newspapers, looking intently at one edition of* The Western Mercury.

TRUDGE So the silly bugger topped himself did a?

JAKE It's what the papers say. There are several reports here in this lot. (*reading*). 'The body was found at ten minutes past ten on February 12th 1901'. Says it here in *The Western Mercury*.

TRUDGE Weird.

JAKE Trevanion made a statement: 'The Trevanions extend their condolences to the wife and family of Mr Cardew. The estate is assisting the authorities with their enquiries in the best way it can'. Look. (*points at a column in the newspaper*). The police here say that no foul play is suspected. They seem to think it was an accident – that he'd lost his footing.

TRUDGE You know what it looks like. We've been down there. You dun't lose your footing . You gotta' go some to do tha'.

JAKE Read this though. This is the kicker. It's a description of the scene shortly afterwards –

TRUDGE *leans in to read the story.*

TRUDGE (*reading*) 'Master R. S. Greenslade – a gardener on the Rosenannon Estate – recalls seeing several pieces of paper floating in the estuary – at first near to the body but then being taken by the tide out to sea'.

JAKE Must be the notes – the pages that he tore out. Only possible explanation idn ut?

TRUDGE So no hanky-panky with Mrs Trevanion then? No love triangle?

JAKE I don't think so – do you?

TRUDGE *shrugs his shoulders.*

TRUDGE So we done now then? You've got what you need?

JAKE I think so. (*takes a deep breath*). It won't be me who's writing it up though. I've had enough of speculation and interpretation.

TRUDGE What ee mean?

JAKE (*sighs*) I've really tried with this doctorate – you know – to get into it – to believe in it – but...

TRUDGE Go on...

JAKE I've decided to step away from it.

TRUDGE (*exasperated*) Whaas' brought that on?

JAKE Dunnaw. These past few days. Just thinking about my life and what I want to do with ut.

TRUDGE You're goin' t'jack ut in?

JAKE Trudge – I dun't see any place fur me with ut. To be successful you've got to be a bit more mainstream.

TRUDGE Cardew is 'mainstream'. Now we've got the Assembly, his face is everywhere. Now we'm a National Minority...

JAKE He doesn't mean a jot to anyone anywhere else. There'll be no job at the end of ut. It's not like we'll have a Department of Celtic Studies... This kind of work, it'll always be tagged onto somethun' else.

TRUDGE You cen't give ut up. You'm the bugger who we wuz all backin' at school – t'show you could get out of the clay works...

JAKE You knaw how tis. You knaw as well as I do Trudge. There idn' any clay work anymore. No Fowey Consuls or any ov ut...

TRUDGE But all the work you've put into ut? All your study idn ut?

JAKE I'll give the Uni library all my notes and files. It wun't go t'waste.

TRUDGE *paces.*

TRUDGE Now this ent because ov what we spoke ov before is ut?

JAKE What?

TRUDGE You knaw... You're difference... That haven't weighed on your mind ave ut?

JAKE No Trudge. Not at all. I know who I am. Always have done. Sometimes you just think you're on the right path, and then, well, you find you're not...

TRUDGE You told Alison yet?

JAKE No. Course not.

TRUDGE But what are ee goin' t'do?

JAKE (*carefree*) Dunnaw. Live on benefits. Screw the government. Be another statistic. One of them not in education, training or employment. Be tested by them buggers at ATOS...

TRUDGE (*interrupting*) You must have a plan? Ever since I've known you Jake, you've always had a plan.

JAKE No – no plan. I just want to let it happen. The way people used to be. (*Beat*). Ph.Ds – they're all about kissing some tutor's arse for three years, submitting papers to obscure journals that no-one ever reads, being obsessed about something that no-one else gives a flying fuck about. (Beat). It's brutal, unforgiving.

TRUDGE (*joking but underplayed*) I've played on-line games that have been the same way.

JAKE No. It's all bollocks Trudge. It's got no meaning. I've evolved. There's goin' to be no more separation from who I am.

TRUDGE (*serious*) It has meaning fur me though. If you becomed Dr Rowe, well, I'd be happy as a sandcart. See, ut would be like everyone of us had made ut – an' got on. Just to prove all them other buggers wrong – they who d'write we off.

JAKE Sorry Trudge.

TRUDGE Well, I'm sorry too.

A pause. Both JAKE *and* TRUDGE *contemplate their futures.*

JAKE Look, in the paper this week – *The Cornish Guardian* – I saw this boat for sale.

TRUDGE Boat?

JAKE A lugger. Like the one on there. (*looks, and notes its disappearance*). Like the one that used to be on there. (*Beat*). I want to work on a boat. Catch fish. Speak Cornish. Do what Cardew really wished for. The rest is just bollocks.

TRUDGE Es. On somethun' like tha' you could swear and cuss as much as you wanted...

JAKE (*dreamily*) You could. You could bait mackerel.

TRUDGE (*more dreamily*) Smoke weed.

JAKE Watch horizons.

TRUDGE Use a g'eat harpoon to kill stuff.

JAKE Forget about everything that didn't matter. Fall into…

TRUDGE …a nice life.

JAKE Could be.

TRUDGE How much do um want fur ut?

JAKE Ten thou.

TRUDGE Christ. (*Beat.*) Still do-able.

JAKE takes out his mobile phone.

JAKE Yeah. Do-able. I got the number. Perhaps I'll give um a ring in a sec. (*Beat*). Look, before tha', I'd better say goodbye to Alison. Thank her fur hosting us…

TRUDGE You carry on boy. I'll sort ut out in here. Dun't ee worry. Aw – don't forget. Grab yer laptop there…

JAKE packs away his laptop.

JAKE (*knowingly*) Anything you want me to say to her?

TRUDGE Na. I dun't think I'm her sort really. She's all… Delectable Duchy… and I'm… I'm… I'm M.C. Kernow… (*Beat*). Go on. I'll catch ee up.

JAKE leaves and shuts the door behind him.

TRUDGE *Tidies up the newspapers and positions items neatly on the table. His eye falls onto the copy of* Bibliotheca Cornubiensis. *He flicks through the pages absent-mindedly until he finds a certain page on which The Sherwood Sermons are mentioned.* TRUDGE *reads the entry slowly and carefully.*

TRUDGE (*out to the hallway, but also to himself*) Jake – don't make that call. Not yet… I think I've found somethun'. The Sermons. They were here. That's what he sought.

TRUDGE *pauses and thinks whether he should tell JAKE. He shuts the book and goes to the door. He almost opens it and then goes back to the book again. He picks up the book and takes it with him. He then rethinks and puts it down again.*

TRUDGE (*to himself*) Na… Leave ut Trudge. Couldn' tell un now. He've made his mind up. Cornish? English? Sometimes, tis best t'say nothing t'all. Let ut go… inta' oblivion like.

TRUDGE *smiles to himself, puts the book down and leaves. He shuts the door behind him. As the transition occurs we hear the following sermon in Cornish, voiced by* CHRISTABELLE:

CHRISTABELLE Ima an papisticall party ow leveral fatell vith an bara ha'n gwyne gwres an very corff ha goose a Grist der an gyrryow a institucyon vttrys gans an pronter in offeren. Ima an apperans an bara han gwyne kefrys ow remainya, in methans y, saw an natur war gy bo an substans an elementys ew veryly chaungys; hag imowns y ow kelwel an chaung ma transubstantio. An dyscas ma yw heb grownd vith in scriptur sans ha pelha contrary ew the reason. An oferen ew sacrament, hag ith ew sacrament signe visibill ha warves a grace spirituall ha wargy. Mar pith an bara han gwyne chaungys in gwir the gorff ha goose Christ, nyna warlergh an papisticall party nyg usy an offeren ow concistia a signes an grace, mas a'n taclow aga honyn. Warlergh an papists rag henna nyns ew sacrament an offeren.

[The Papists say that in the mass, the bread and wine, by the words of institution uttered by the priest, verily become the body and blood of Christ. The appearance of both bread and wine remain, they say, but the internal nature or substance of the elements is indeed changed; and this change they call transubstantiation. This doctrine is without warrant in scripture and is contrary to reason. The mass is a sacrament and a sacrament is an outward and visible sign of an inward and spiritual grace. If, however, the bread and wine are verily changed into the body and blood of Christ, the mass does not consist of the signs of the grace but consists of the things themselves. The mass therefore according to the papists is not a sacrament.]

Epilogue

The last thing we hear is Actor 1 saying the following lines as the character of TRUDGE. *These are thoughtful and laconic*

86

TRUDGE When you're a kid, they tell you to grow up, get a job, get married, get a house, have kids and that's it. *(Beat)*. But the truth is that the world is so much stranger than that. It's so much darker, so much more mad and crazy... and so much better.

– END –